VEGAN RUSTIC COOKING

COOKING

Through The Seasons

Diana White

Permanent Publications

THE QUEEN'S AWARDS
FOR ENTERPRISE:
SUSTAINABLE DEVELOPMENT
2008

Published by
Permanent Publications
Hyden House Ltd
The Sustainability Centre
East Meon
Hampshire GU32 1HR
United Kingdom
Tel: 01730 823 311
Fax: 01730 823 322
Overseas: (international code +44 - 1730)
Email: enquiries@permaculture.co.uk
Web: www.permaculture.co.uk

First distributed b.y the Vegan-Organic Network 2002 (no ISBN)
Revised, expanded and illustrated 2006
© 2006 Diana White, reprinted 2008, 2010
p.a.white@ukgateway.net

The right of Diana White to be identified as the author of this work has been asserted by her in accordance with the Copyrights, Designs and Patents Act 1998.

Designed and typeset by Tim Harland

Illustrated by Richard Watts

FSC
Mixed Sources
Product group from well-managed
forests and other controlled sources
Cert no. SGS-COC-2953
www.fsc.org
© 1996 Forest Stewardship Council

Printed by CPI Antony Rowe Ltd, Chippenham, Wiltshire

Printed on paper from mixed sources
certified by the Forest Stewardship Council

British Library Cataloguing-in-Publication Data.
A catalogue record for this book is available from the British Library.

ISBN 978-1-85623-034-6

Contents

About the Author

The author was a vegetarian for 23 years and for the last 14 has been a vegan. She and her husband grow their own fruit and vegetables vegan-organically and to some extent the book grew out of the vegetable plot, as recipes were created to utilise the seasonal produce. The author is a trustee of the charity, The Vegan-Organic Network.

About the Artist

The artist, Richard Watts, is a vegan and has an honours degree in illustration from the University of Lincoln. Richard's website is www.godfist.com

Acknowledgements

Many thanks go to Richard Watts, Barbara Marshall, Ziggy Woodward and Peter White for their assistance in the production of this book.

Dedications

This book is dedicated to the Vegan-Organic Network (VON), registered charity 1080847. The charity was established to provide education and research into vegan-organic principles. VON's magazine Growing Green International is circulated worldwide and the charity has many supporters in the UK and elsewhere. The charity's website is www.veganorganic.net

This book is also dedicated to the author's mother, to the earth herself, and to all animals everywhere.

The Big Picture

This cook book contains inspiring recipes based on sound nutritional principles. What we eat not only affects our own health but also has a profound impact on our planet and all its inhabitants.

We hear regular dire reports about the environment and food shortages. Global warming, land degradation, species extinction, famines and pollution appear as news items almost daily. There is no doubt that our dependence on animal farming plays a huge part in creating these problems.

Most farm land in the West is used for livestock rearing, but it is not sufficient, so many countries import plant crops as fodder from the developing world – fodder that takes up huge areas of land in the poorest parts of the globe where people are starving. The local farmers are left to scrape a living on the margins while the rich West deprives their countries of prime agricultural land in order to feed its own farmed animals. Yet 24 million people starve to death every year and every three seconds a child dies of malnutrition.

The question that must be asked is, can the world support two population explosions, that of humans and that of animals deliberately and unnecessarily bred for food? Livestock consume more protein and calories than they produce. A typical European omnivorous diet requires many times the amount of land needed for a varied plant-based diet. A plant-based diet could feed the world.

Annually 200 million tons of effluent are produced by British farm animals, much of which, along with other pollutants, ends up in our rivers and the sea.

A more natural environment without the heavy burden of farmed animals would be splendid, especially if this were to be combined with the elimination of chemical inputs. The beauty of nature would surround us, as trees, wild flowers, birds and all of creation would once more emerge in their full glory.

Fresh water is a vital but diminishing resource, but irrigation is necessary for all forms of agriculture. It has been estimated by Professor D. Pimentel of Cornell University that it takes 500 litres of water to produce 1kg of potatoes, 900 litres per kg of wheat, 3,500 litres per kg of edible chicken flesh and a huge 100,000 litres per kg of beef. Even the more conservative estimates of water usage accept that, for example, beef production requires many times more water than wheat.

The roots of these problems are not just to be found in some remote part of the world but are also in our own back yard.

The Vegan-Organic Network (VON) says: human development is a progression in which we all have a part to play. One line of progress we should now work towards is away from destructive conventional chemical agriculture to vegan-organic agriculture (ordinary organic agriculture is only marginally more animal-friendly than conventional farming). The only clear and unequivocal ethical position is that of vegans who rule out the rearing of farm animals altogether. There are vegan-organic farms all over the world growing wholesome food ethically and sustainably, thereby providing a practical example of 'Stockfree' agriculture.

Vegan-organics is the answer to the huge problems caused by animal based agriculture. Vegan-organics is any system of cultivation that avoids artificial chemicals and sprays, livestock manures and animal remains from slaughterhouses, fish processing, etc. Alternatively, fertility is maintained by vegetable compost, green manures, crop rotation, mulches, undersowing and any other method that is sustainable, ecologically viable and not dependent upon farm animal exploitation. These methods have been demonstrated on vegan-organic farms around the world and will ensure long term fertility and wholesome food for this and future generations.

VON has developed the worlds first Stockfree-Organic Standards, whereby farmers who wish to adopt animal-free environmentally-friendly organic cultivation will be able to obtain both the Soil Association and the Stockfree-Organic symbol. Consumers will now know that produce bearing the distinctive Stockfree-Organic Symbol has been grown to these high standards. With farming in crisis VON has an ethical and pragmatic message that will meet this challenge and carry food production into a new era. Stockfree-Organics embraces non-violence towards all life, providing a model and a catalyst for social, economic and cultural change; change that is essential if we are to have a future.

If time allows it is good for individuals to grow some of their own fruit and vegetables vegan-organically. This is a rewarding creative activity, which apart from giving fresh air and exercise also invigorates the mind. Just growing a few seasonal items yourself can save on food miles and packaging, making you less dependent on foreign imports. Also the flavour, purity, and nutritional value of home-grown produce is usually higher than the commercially grown equivalent.

Joining VON will give you access to advice and information about how to 'grow your own' through its journal *Growing Green International*, information sheets and in many other ways. You will also learn about visits to vegan farms, how to volunteer and gain experience by working on them. VON welcomes support from all who are concerned with ethical cultivation and social justice. Even if you have no opportunity to grow your own food your support will accelerate the process of getting vegan-organic food in the shops! Your membership will help VON's training and education programme through its Student Bursary Fund. By joining you will learn of the worldwide advances in animal-free growing and will be updated about the increasing number of farms that supply food grown to Stockfree-Organic standards.

To find out more about VON see www.veganorganic.net, or ring (UK) 0845 223 5232 (local rate).

Cooking Ingredients

1. When using tofu, always try to obtain it made with nigari as this has a superior texture and flavour to the one made with calcium; besides, there are plenty of calcium rich foods in this book. Nigari contains magnesium, iron and other minerals and tofu made with it lends itself nicely to many dishes.

2. Always use a good quality tamari soya sauce or shoyu soya sauce.

3. Fine sea salt is meant wherever salt is mentioned.

4. Sea vegetables should be eaten regularly, but because of their strength, in small portions. They add valuable nutrition and flavour and are a powerful tool to detoxify the body. Eat a variety to ensure a wide range of vitamins and minerals etc; clean as per the instructions on the packet.

5. Dried pulses should be cooked according to the instructions on the packet.

6. A quality vegetable fat spread/margarine to use is one made with rapeseed oil, as it is a good source of omega-3 fatty acids.

Eating Seasonally

These recipes vary from strong autumn/winter recipes such as cottage pie with gravy and warm puddings, right through to summer salads and trifle; they are most enjoyable and health giving when eaten at the appropriate time of the year.

Measurements

For measuring out ingredients use only teaspoons and tablespoons specially standardised for this purpose. Both metric and American equivalent measurements are given throughout. The cup sizes mentioned are American standard ones; 1 cup equals 240ml. All these measuring utensils can be found in many cook shops.

Servings

Most of the recipes are for 2 or 4 servings. A recipe with 4 servings could have its ingredients halved for 2 people. A single person could halve a 2 servings recipe; and could likewise halve a 4 servings recipe and eat it over 2 days.

Cleaning of
Shop or Home Grown Vegetables

Scrub all root vegetables and potatoes with a stainless steel pan scourer or a vegetable brush, removing any bad bits, then rinse.

For all other vegetables, discard bad bits and place in a sink or large bowl (leeks should be chopped first). Submerge in cold water, sprinkle liberally with salt and swish them about a little. Take out and rinse twice in fresh cold water.

Oven Temperatures

Gas mark	°F	°C
1	275	140
2	300	150
3	325	170
4	350	180
5	375	190
6	400	200
7	425	220
8	450	230
9	475	240

Availability of Produce

Products such as miso, sea vegetables and tamari are becoming more readily available. If, however, you cannot find a local stockist, visit your nearest town or city and make a bulk purchase, checking that the sell by dates are long running. Alternatively, look on the Internet or in a veggie magazine for stockists.

SOUPS

Corn Chowder

3 large or 4 small servings
2 tablespoons of rapeseed oil
2 large onions chopped small
750g / 1lb 10oz of potatoes diced
3 corn cobs, husked, remove the corn from the cobs
250ml / 1 cup of soya milk
½ teaspoon of paprika
1 tablespoon of tamari soya sauce
salt and pepper to taste
garnish of rocket or watercress chopped

Place the oil in a large pan. Add the onions and potatoes and stew until the onions soften slightly, keep stirring to prevent sticking.

Add the corn, milk, 550ml / 2⅓ cups of water and the paprika. Bring to boil and simmer until the onions and potatoes are tender, stirring from time to time.

Add the tamari plus salt and pepper to taste mixing in well, simmer for 1 minute more.

Serve topped with the rocket or watercress and with crusty bread if wished.

Leek & Potato Soup

4 large or 6 small servings
1kg / 2lb 4oz of potatoes chopped small
3 medium leeks finely chopped
375ml / 1½ cups of soya milk
3 tablespoons of shoyu soya sauce
½ teaspoon of paprika
salt and pepper to taste
garnish of parsley or watercress chopped (discard
stems)

Place the potatoes and leeks in a large pan with 1 litre / 4¼ cups of water. Bring to boil then turn to simmer and place the lid on. Cook until tender, approximately 10 minutes.

Drain the stock off into a jug and mash the vegetables. Add the milk, shoyu and paprika and enough of the stock to make a thick soup consistency. Bring to boil stirring thoroughly. Then simmer for 1 minute, seasoning with salt and pepper.

Garnish each portion with the parsley or watercress and serve with croutons if wished.

Jerusalem Artichoke Soup

Serves 4
2 tablespoons of sesame oil
400g / 1lb of Jerusalem artichokes (no need to peel)
cut into slivers
2 large red onions sliced into slim wedges
400g / 1lb of potatoes diced
1½ tablespoons of nori flakes or 1 teaspoon of sea
vegetable granules, e.g. wild wrack
1 tablespoon of barley miso or yeast / vegetable extract
salt and pepper to taste

Sauté the artichokes and potatoes in the oil in a large pan for 5 minutes, turning regularly to prevent sticking. Add the onions and sauté 3 minutes more.

Add 1 litre / 4¼ cups of water and the nori flakes or the granules. Bring to boil and simmer until tender stirring from time to time. Then add the miso plus salt and pepper to taste mixing well in.

Serve with crusty bread if wished.

Parsnip & Blackeyed Bean Soup

Sweet and nourishing.

Serves 4 as a meal
250g / 1½ cups of dried blackeyed beans
optional: 9cm / 3½ inch strip of kombu cut small
4 large parsnips
2 large carrots
2 large onions
large bunch of cabbage greens
all the above vegetables chopped small
1½ tablespoons of barley miso or yeast / vegetable extract
salt and pepper to taste
optional: capers

Place the beans, sea vegetable (if used), parsnips and carrots into a large pan with enough water to cover.

Bring to boil and simmer until tender, keeping the water level just above the ingredients.

When cooked add the greens and onions and simmer for a further 7 minutes.

Drain the liquid into a jug and mash the ingredients roughly, then return the liquid and add the miso stirring well in.

Simmer for a few more minutes, gradually adding water until the required thickness is reached (this should be quite thick soup). Season with salt and pepper.

If wished sprinkle capers over each helping. Serve with crusty bread or croutons if desired.

Cream of Pea Soup

Serves 2
410g can / 1¾ cups of organic processed peas; do not
drain (it is essential to use organic as standard canned
peas are just not good enough)
1 tablespoon of shoyu soya sauce
1 teaspoon of sea vegetable granules, e.g. wild wrack
½ mug / ¾ cup of soya milk
salt and pepper if wished

Empty the peas and their liquid into a pan and roughly mash with a
potato masher.

Add the shoyu, sea vegetable granules and milk plus ½ mug / ¾ cup of
water. Bring to boil and simmer for a few minutes mixing all well in.
Add salt and pepper if wished.

Serve with crusty bread or croutons if desired.

Flask Soup

Good to take outdoors on a cold day.

Serves 2
1½ tablespoons of barley miso
1 teaspoon of sea vegetable granules, e.g. wild wrack
1 teaspoon of finely chopped root ginger
1 tablespoon of oat flakes (not whole or jumbo oats)
optional: 2 large shiitake mushrooms, stems
discarded, cut into small pieces / 2 pieces of snow
dried tofu broken into very small pieces

Assemble the above together in a large thermos flask. Boil 2 mugs of water in a kettle, pour over the ingredients, screw on the lid and gently turn the flask upside down a few times to mix.

Leave for 20 minutes or longer before consuming and take a spoon for any chunky bits. Shake gently before opening.

Japanese Noodle Broth

Here is a dish with a difference, that is easy to make.

2 main meal sized or 4 small servings
225g / ½lb of udon noodles
sprinkling of salt
a few strands of hijiki or arame sea vegetable
1 medium carrot cut into thin sticks
2 to 3 pieces of snow tofu broken into bits and
sprinkled with tamari soya sauce
1 large mug / 1½ cups of cooked beans
3 dried shiitake mushrooms cut small, stalks discarded
½ tablespoon of finely chopped root ginger
1 tablespoon of barley miso or yeast / vegetable extract
bunch of spring onions or 1 large leek, including any
decent green parts, chopped

Place 1 litre / 4¼ cups of water into a large pan and bring to boil. Add the noodles, salt, sea vegetable, carrot, tofu, beans, mushrooms, ginger and leek (if used).

Simmer with the lid partly on until the noodles are tender, do not drain. The broth should be nearly halfway up the noodles when they are cooked; if this is not the case then add a little more water and re-heat to simmering.

Add the miso and spring onions (if used). Simmer strongly for 2 minutes and keep mixing all well in. Eat with a fork and spoon.

Minestrone

Nice to enjoy with friends.

Serves 4 as a meal
200g / 1¼ cups of dried chickpeas soaked overnight

Place the beans and their soaking water in a large pan and cook until tender, keeping the water level just above the beans, do not drain.

> 2 tablespoons of olive oil
> 2 large carrots chopped
> 4 medium potatoes diced small
> 2 large onions chopped
> large bunch of cabbage greens chopped small
> 400g can / 1¾ cups of premium tomatoes chopped
> 1 tablespoon of marjoram or oregano
> 2 to 3 garlic cloves crushed
> 150g / 6oz of spaghetti broken into small pieces
> 3 tablespoons of tamari soya sauce
> salt and pepper to taste
> *optional*: small packet of ground almonds

Whilst the beans are cooking sauté the carrots and potatoes in a large non-stick frying pan with the olive oil. After 5 minutes add the onions and cook for 5 minutes longer, set aside.

When the beans are cooked add the sautéed vegetables to them, plus the cabbage, tomatoes, marjoram, garlic and 1 litre / 4¼ cups of water. Bring to boil mixing all well in. Simmer strongly for a couple of minutes and then add the spaghetti and cook until the pasta is tender.

By this time the soup will be nice and thick, if too thick pour in a *little* water. Add the tamari plus salt and pepper to taste stirring well in.

If wished sprinkle a little ground almond over the top of each portion and serve with crusty bread.

Creamy Butterbean Soup

A strong rich dish.

Serves 4 as a meal
600g / 3¼ cups of dried butterbeans
9cm / 3½ inch strip of kombu cut up small

Cook the above in a large pan until very soft, keeping the water level just above the beans, do not drain.

2 medium leeks finely chopped including decent green parts
1½ tablespoons of rice miso or yeast / vegetable extract
150g / 1¾ cups of ground almonds
salt and pepper
small bunch of parsley chopped (discard stems)

Add the leeks to the butterbeans (but no more water) and place the lid on. Simmer for 7 minutes, stirring occasionally to prevent sticking.

Add the miso and ground almonds and mix all well in together. Then add more water if necessary to make a thick creamy soup. Simmer for a couple of minutes adding salt and pepper to taste.

Serve garnished with the parsley and if desired, crusty bread.

Rice & Yellow Pea Pottage

Sturdy and warming for a bitter day.

> **Serves 4 as a meal**
> 300g / 1²/₃ cups of dried yellow split peas
> 200g / 1 cup of whole short grain rice
> *optional*: 9cm / 3½ inch strip of kombu cut small

Cook the peas, rice and sea vegetable (if used) in a large pan until tender, stirring occasionally to prevent sticking. Keep the water level just above the ingredients, do not drain.

> 2 tablespoons of rapeseed oil
> 400g / 14oz of potatoes diced
> 2 medium leeks including any decent green parts
> thinly sliced
> 2 garlic cloves crushed
> 1½ tablespoons of barley miso or yeast / vegetable
> extract
> 1 tablespoon of sage
> salt and pepper

Whilst the peas and rice are cooking sauté the potatoes in the oil, in a large non-stick frying pan for 3 minutes. Then add the leeks and garlic and sauté for 5 minutes longer.

When the rice and peas are tender add the vegetables, barley miso, sage and 650ml / 2¾ cups of water. Bring to boil then simmer until the vegetables are tender, stirring from time to time to prevent sticking. Season with salt and pepper to taste.

Scotch Broth

Serves 4 as a meal
50g / 1 cup of pot barley

Cook the barley in a large pan until tender (approximately 50 minutes) keeping the water level just above the barley. Stir occasionally to prevent sticking.

>	2 tablespoons of rapeseed oil
>	400g / 14oz of swede / rutabaga diced small
>	400g / 14oz of potatoes diced medium
>	3 large sticks of celery chopped small
>	2 medium carrots chopped
>	2 medium leeks sliced including any decent green parts
>	1½ teaspoons of sea vegetable granules, e.g. wild wrack
>	1½ tablespoons of barley miso or yeast / vegetable extract
>	salt and pepper to taste
>	small carton of natural soya yoghurt

Sauté the swede / rutabaga in the oil, in a large non-stick frying pan for 5 minutes, then add the potatoes, celery and carrots and sauté for a further 7 minutes.

When the barley is cooked do not drain; add the sautéed vegetables mixing in. Add the leeks, sea vegetable granules, miso and 1 litre / 4¼ cups of water. Bring to boil, then simmer until tender stirring occasionally to prevent sticking. Season with salt and pepper to taste, stirring well in.

Serve with a blob or two of yoghurt in the centre of each portion and crusty bread if wished.

Aduki Bean Pottage

A substantial soup to keep you going for many hours.

> **Serves 4 as a meal**
> 250g / 1⅓ cups of dried aduki beans soaked overnight
> 2 large potatoes diced
> *optional*: 9cm / 3½ inch strip of wakame
> (or use 1 or 2 strands) cut up small

Cook the adukis in their soaking water with the potatoes and sea vegetable (if used) in a large pan until tender, keeping the water level just above the ingredients, do not drain.

> 2 large onions chopped
> large bunch of cabbage greens chopped
> 2 medium carrots grated
> 1 teaspoon of turmeric
> 100g / ½ cup of tomato puree
> 1½ tablespoons of barley miso
> 1 tablespoon of cider vinegar
> 1 tablespoon of sage
> salt and pepper

When the beans are tender, add the rest of the ingredients plus 1 litre / 4¼ cups of water and bring to boil, mixing all well in. Then simmer until tender (approximately 7 minutes) stirring regularly. Add salt and pepper to taste.

Serve with crusty bread if wished.

FILLINGS FOR SANDWICHES, TOAST & BAKED POTATOES

Baked Tofu / Tempeh

Ideal for sandwiches.

> sesame oil
> small packet of tofu or tempeh cut into bite sized
> pieces
> tamari soya sauce
> *optional*: paprika or cayenne pepper

Lightly grease a non-stick oven tray with the oil and fill with the tofu or tempeh. Sprinkle tamari and if wished one of the options over all the pieces and bake at gas 8 / 450°F for 15 minutes, turning the tray halfway through the cooking time.

Butterbean Pate

420g can / 1½ cups of butterbeans drained
1 teaspoon of olive oil
½ tablespoon of barley miso
sprinkling of pepper
3 tablespoons of natural soya yoghurt

Place all the above in a flat bottomed dish, Mash well in with the back of a fork, placing the index finger in the centre of the fork head as you do so.

Suitable for serving with a green and red salad (include spring onions / scallions) on 'wrap and roll' flat bread or pitta / pocket bread.

Creamy Savoury Topping

1 tablespoon of olive oil
7 tablespoons of ground almonds
5 tablespoons of natural soya yoghurt
½ tablespoon of shoyu soya sauce
sprinkling of salt
optional: sprinkling of dried chives or nori flakes

Mix all the above together in a bowl.

4 large, medium thick slices of whole wheat bread
2 large tomatoes chopped

Toast the bread on both sides then cover with the creamy topping and place the tomatoes on top. Grill / broil for 20 seconds only and serve.

Hummus

410g can / 1⅓ cups of chickpeas drained
1 teaspoon of olive oil
2 garlic cloves crushed
juice of half a lemon
1½ tablespoons of sesame seed paste

Place the chickpeas in a flat bottomed dish. Sauté the garlic lightly in the oil. Add to the chickpeas along with the lemon juice and sesame seed paste. Mash all well in together with the back of a fork, placing the index finger in the centre of the fork head as you do so. Add a little water to the hummus as you mash, to avoid it becoming too dry.

Red Bean Pate

420g can / 1½ cups of red kidney beans drained
½ tablespoon of barley miso
½ tablespoon of chilli sauce
1 tablespoon of tomato puree
1 tablespoon of olive oil

Place all the above in a flat bottomed dish. Mash well in with the back of a fork, placing the index finger in the centre of the fork head as you do so.

Suitable for serving with a green salad and chopped spring onions / scallions on a 'wrap and roll' flat bread or in pitta / pocket bread.

Scrambled Tofu

1 tablespoon of sesame oil
280g / 1¾ cups of tofu cubed
1½ tablespoons of shoyu soya sauce
a few spring onions / scallions including green parts or
chives chopped

Place all the above (except the onions / scallions or chives) in a dish and mash thoroughly with the back of a fork. Sauté for a few minutes in a non-stick frying pan, then add the onions / scallions or chives and cook for 1 minute more.

Serve warm.

Sesame Seed Paste & Tamari Topping

Toast some slices of whole wheat bread and cover with stoneground, dark sesame seed paste. Sprinkle tamari soya sauce over the top and blend with the paste. Serve immediately.

Alfalfa & Yoghurt Filler

3 tablespoons of alfalfa seeds (this amount will provide quite a lot of sprouts)
large plastic mineral water bottle with the top quarter cut off
muslin or similar cloth to cover bottle top rubber band
500g / 2 cups of natural soya yoghurt

Soak the seeds over night in the bottle. The next day place the cloth over the bottle opening and secure with the rubber band.

Rinse morning, afternoon and night, for 3 days. Always leave in a slightly tilted position over a dish (to ensure drainage) in a mildly warm place.

On the fourth day if the sprouted part of the seed is at least 25mm / 1 inch long it is ready for use. If not continue the rinsing process for another day.

If you wish these sprouts to green up, once they start to show, leave them in the light.

If filling bread use pitta / pocket bread and cover it thinly with vegetable fat spread and fill with the sprouts and a helping of yoghurt. Soft bread will absorb the yoghurt so unless eaten immediately after making do not use.

Any leftover sprouts can be stored in the fridge for 3 days, rinse and drain once daily.

Banana & Sesame Seed Spread

Mash a banana and 1½ tablespoons of stoneground, dark sesame seed paste all together with the back of a fork, adding a little salt if there is none in the paste. Spread on bread or toast and serve immediately.

Tofu Pate

280g / 1¾ cups of tofu cubed
2 teaspoons of commercial mustard
1 tablespoon of sesame oil
1 tablespoon of tamari soya sauce

Place all the above in a dish and mash thoroughly with the back of a fork.

Avocado Pate

An easy to make treat.

>1 medium avocado (ripe but not over ripe)
>1 tablespoon of cider vinegar
>sprinkling of salt and pepper

Scoop out the flesh of the avocado and place in a bowl. Add the other ingredients and mash well with the back of a fork. Spread on toast and serve immediately.

Guacamole

Great for a hot summer's day.

Serves 2
2 medium avocados (ripe when the flesh slightly gives
on pressing with your fingers)
5 tablespoons of vegan commercial mayonnaise
1 tablespoon of cider vinegar
¼ teaspoon of cayenne pepper
optional: sprinkling of salt

Remove the flesh from the avocados and place in a flat bottomed dish
along with the other ingredients and mash well with the back of a fork.

Serve at the centre of a salad along with crusty bread or on toast.

The guacamole will keep for at least 24 hours if it is placed in an
earthenware dish and covered with baking foil; press the foil well down
onto the pate to make it airtight and refrigerate.

Mushroom Pate

Strong and nourishing.

> 1½ tablespoons of olive oil
> 200g / ½lb of mushrooms finely sliced
> 1 tablespoon of barley miso
> 1 tablespoon of whole wheat flour

Sauté the mushrooms in the oil, in a large non-stick frying pan, for a couple of minutes. Add the miso and cook 2 minutes longer, mashing the mushrooms roughly with the back of a fork. Finally sprinkle with the flour and cook for a further 2 or 3 minutes, continuing to mash roughly.

Olive Pate

400g can / 1½ cups of pitted black olives drained
(reserve the brine)
1½ tablespoons of olive oil
1½ tablespoons of whole wheat flour

Chop the olives into bits. Place in a large non-stick frying pan with the oil and sauté for 1 minute. Then sprinkle with the flour plus 2 or 3 tablespoons of the brine and continue to cook for a few more minutes, roughly mashing the olives with the back of a fork as you do so.

Grated carrot goes well with this pate.

Red Onion Pickle With Miso

1 large red onion
cider vinegar
unpasteurised barley miso

Cut the onion into fine semi circles. Place in a flat bottomed dish. Pour in enough vinegar to comfortably cover the base. Toss the onion in the vinegar until well coated and place in the fridge.

The next day, turn the onion over with your fingers, so that the top goes to the bottom and place back in the fridge. Start using the following day; keeps for 3 days more in the fridge.

Cover some bread with vegetable fat spread and the miso and place the onion pickle on top.

Baked Onions

1½ tablespoons of sesame oil
2 large onions chopped chunky
salt

Mix the oil and onion together thoroughly, then spread out on a non-stick oven tray and sprinkle with salt. Bake at gas 8 / 450ºF for 30 minutes, turning the tray halfway through the cooking time.

SAUCES

Basic Sweet & Sour Sauce

Serves 4
1 tablespoon of olive oil
1 large onion finely chopped
350ml / 1½ cups of apple juice
2 tablespoons of corn flour
2 tablespoons of tamari soya sauce

Sauté the onion in the oil in a large non-stick frying pan. When tender add the apple juice. Blend the corn flour with the tamari until smooth and add to the pan mixing in thoroughly. Gradually bring to boil stirring constantly then simmer for a couple of minutes stirring regularly.

Serve over bakes and vegetables.

Carrot Sauce

Serves 4
3 medium carrots grated
50g / ¼ cup of tomato puree
2 tablespoons of corn flour
2 tablespoons of shoyu soya sauce

Place the first 2 ingredients in a pan and add 500ml / 2¼ cups of stock or water stirring well in. Put the corn flour in a mug with the shoyu and blend together. Add to the sauce mixing in thoroughly. Place on a high heat and stir well while bringing to boil, then reduce heat to simmer for a couple of minutes.

Can be served over bakes.

Creamy Savoury Sauce

Serves 4

4 tablespoons of whole wheat flour
²/₃ mug / 1 cup of ground almonds
2 tablespoons of tamari soya sauce
optional: ½ teaspoon of nutmeg or mustard powder or
a few grindings of black pepper
350ml / 1½ cups of soya milk
salt to taste

Place the first 3 ingredients in a pan plus an option if required and gradually add the soya milk, mixing to a creamy consistency. Then add 350ml / 1½ cups of water and place on a high heat, stir constantly with a wooden spatula until the sauce thickens. Then turn to simmer for 1 minute adding salt and mixing well in.

Serve over vegetables.

Mushroom Sauce

Serves 4
1 tablespoon of olive oil
225g / ½lb of mushrooms finely chopped
1½ tablespoons of barley miso
2 tablespoons of whole wheat flour

Sauté the mushrooms in the oil, in a large non-stick frying pan, for a couple of minutes. Add the miso and cook for 2 minutes longer, mashing the mushrooms roughly using the back of a fork.

Scatter the flour over the mixture and cook for a further minute, continuing to mash roughly. Finally add 300ml / 1¼ cups of water and gradually bring to boil stirring constantly. Then simmer for 3 minutes stirring regularly, adding a little more water if the mixture becomes too thick.

Serve over baked potatoes, or use in place of gravy.

Rich Lentil Sauce

Serves 4
See Moussaka Vegan Style on page 88 for this sauce.

Lentil Sauce

Serves 4
250g / 1⅓ cups of dried lentils (not red)
optional: 9cm / 3½ inch strip of wakame (or 1 or 2 fine strands) cut up small
1 large onion chopped
1½ teaspoons of marjoram
1 tablespoon of barley miso or yeast / vegetable extract
salt
1 tablespoon of corn flour

Cook the lentils and sea vegetable, if used, in a medium pan until tender; keeping the water level just above the pulses, do not drain.

When the lentils are cooked add the onion, marjoram and miso (but no more water) and cook until the onion is tender. Then add salt to taste. Put the corn flour in a mug and blend with 2 tablespoons of water; add to the sauce mixing in well. Bring to boil stirring constantly, then simmer for a couple of minutes stirring regularly. Add a little more water if the sauce is too thick.

Serve over roasted root vegetables or hot pot vegetables.

Apple Sauce

Serves 4 to 6
4 cooking apples or equivalent strong flavoured dessert
apples diced, discard the centres
juice of 1 lemon
if using cooking apples, 1 tablespoon of muscovado sugar
optional: korma curry powder

Put the apples and lemon juice in a pan with 150ml / $^2/_3$ cup of water, place the lid on and steam with the heat at $^2/_3$ its full blast for 3 minutes. When cooked, turn to a gentle simmer adding the sugar and a little curry powder if required, then mash.

Serve as an accompaniment to bean dishes or with bakes and roasts.

Creamy Nori Sauce

Serves 4
4 tablespoons of whole wheat flour
2 tablespoons of nori flakes
1⅓ tablespoons of barley miso
300ml / 1¼ cups of soya milk
salt and pepper to taste

Place the first 3 ingredients in a pan and gradually add the milk, mixing to a creamy consistency. Then add 350ml / 1½ cups of stock or water and place on a high heat, stirring constantly until the sauce thickens. Then turn to simmer for a couple of minutes, adding salt and pepper to taste and stirring well.

Serve with bakes or grain and vegetable meals.

Gravy (light)

Serves 4
5 tablespoons of whole wheat flour
620ml / 2½ cups of stock
shoyu soya sauce

Place the flour in a pan and gradually mix in the stock. Place on a high heat stirring constantly until the gravy thickens. Then simmer for a couple of minutes adding shoyu to taste; stir regularly.

Gravy (rich)

Serves 4
4 tablespoons of whole wheat flour
250ml / 1 cup of soya milk
3 tablespoons of barley miso
optional: dashes of herbs, salt, sautéed onion, a few mushrooms finely chopped

Place the flour in a pan and gradually mix in the milk. Then add the miso and 400ml / 1¾ cups of stock or water. Place on a high heat stirring constantly. When the gravy has thickened turn to simmer for a couple of minutes stirring regularly. If necessary, gradually add more stock until the required consistency is reached.

If options are required, add once you have turned the heat to simmer, and cook for a few minutes longer, stirring regularly.

Spicy Nut Butter Sauce

Serves 2
1 tablespoon of olive oil
1 large onion finely chopped
5 tablespoons of oat flakes (not jumbo or whole oats)
4 tablespoons of peanut butter
1 teaspoon of muscovado sugar
$2/3$ teaspoon of deep red paprika
$2/3$ teaspoon of ground nutmeg
1 tablespoon of shoyu soya sauce

Sauté the onion in the oil in a pan until tender. Take off the heat and add the oats, peanut butter, muscovado sugar, paprika, nutmeg and shoyu and roughly mix together.

Gradually add 400ml / 1¾ cups of stock or water, mixing well in. Place on a high heat and bring to boil, stirring as you do so. Then turn to simmer for a couple of minutes, stirring from time to time. Add salt to taste if there is none in the peanut butter.

If wished, serve over pasta and vegetables or rice and vegetables.

MAIN MEALS

Rich Green Leafy Vegetables

These should be eaten daily. Avoid over cooking them otherwise they will lose colour, nutrition and flavour. Given below is a list to choose from:

Kale
Brussels sprouts
Brussels sprout tops
Turnip greens
Traditional cos or webb lettuce
Watercress
Rocket
Parsley
Chives
Leeks with plenty of green leaves
Spring onions with their green ends
Purple sprouting broccoli and leaves
Swede tops
Cabbage greens (spring greens)
Any other cabbage with a good supply of rich green leaves
Oriental greens
Young beetroot / beet tops
Spinach } once or twice a week only
Swiss chard

How To Steam Vegetables

If using hard vegetables such as carrots or swede, chop them into small pieces and place in a large pan with 250ml / 1 cup of water.

For softer vegetables such as greens or cauliflower, chop small and place in a large pan with 150ml / ²/₃ cup of water. Do not fill the pan more than half full of vegetables.

Place the lid on and set the heat to ¾ of its full power. Soft vegetables will take about 5 minutes and hard ones about 10 minutes or a little longer.

Do not leave the pan unattended, as it will soon dry out and burn. Add a little more water if necessary. At the end of the cooking time turn the heat down low and keep your distance as you lift the lid.

Drain and if wished add a knob of vegetable fat spread plus salt and pepper, and mix in.

If you want to steam hard and soft vegetables together then simply start off with the hard ones in 250ml of water and steam for 7 minutes, then add the softer ones and continue to steam for approximately 5 more minutes.

Rice & Chickpea Patties

Satisfying and tasty

Serves 4
400g can / 1⅓ cups of chickpeas drained
250g / 1½ cups of leftover whole grain cooked rice
1⅓ tablespoons of nori flakes or herbs of choice
5 tablespoons of ground almonds
4 tablespoons of strong whole wheat flour
2 tablespoons of shoyu soya sauce

Drain the chickpeas and mash with the back of a fork, placing the index finger in the centre of the fork head as you do so. Add the rest of the ingredients to the chickpeas and mix together thoroughly. Make into 8 patties.

Sauté in a large, oiled, non-stick frying pan until golden brown on both sides.

Serving suggestion: In warm weather serve with a salad and crusty bread; in cold weather serve with roasted vegetables and sauerkraut or apple sauce (*see page 40*).

Goulash

Most enjoyable at any time of the year.

Serves 4
3 tablespoons of olive oil
400g / 2 cups of whole short grain rice
2 bay leaves
1½ teaspoons of rosemary
1 teaspoon of cayenne pepper
400g can / 1¾ cups of premium tomatoes chopped

summer: 450g / 1lb of runner beans / string beans sliced
other seasons: 2 medium carrots chopped

summer: 3 courgettes / zucchini sliced
other seasons: large bunch of cabbage greens chopped
2 large onions chopped
2 410g cans / 2⅔ cups of chickpeas drained
3 to 4 tablespoons of shoyu soya sauce
500g / 2 cups of natural soya yoghurt

Place 2 tablespoons of the oil, rice, bay leaves, rosemary and cayenne in a large pan and sauté for a few minutes, stirring all well in.

Add the tomatoes and 625ml / 2¾ cups of water. Bring to boil, then simmer very gently for 20 minutes with the lid on. Add the runner beans / string beans or carrots and simmer for 10 minutes longer with the lid on.

Meanwhile, place the remaining tablespoon of oil in a large non-stick frying pan along with the courgettes / zucchini or greens, plus the onions, and sauté until half tender. You might need to add a little water to the greens if they are too dry.

When the rice has cooked for 30 minutes, add the rest of the vegetables, chick peas, shoyu and a mug / 1¼ cups of water. Mix all well in and bring to boil; simmer strongly with the lid on for approximately 10 minutes, by which time most of the liquid should have been absorbed. Do not let the goulash dry out; add a little more water if necessary.

Serve with the yoghurt spooned over each portion.

Quick Savoury Pancakes

Using the same batter mix and cooking method as in the recipe on page 132, pancakes can be made by incorporating one or two of the following into the batter before cooking, but do not overload, or the pancakes may break up:

Serves 2
baby can of sweet corn drained
1 teaspoon of herbs
4 tablespoons of alfalfa sprouts
3 tablespoons of sunflower seeds
sprinkling of cayenne or deep red paprika
3 tablespoons of ground almonds
1 tablespoon of nori flakes
4 spring onions / scallions or a few fresh chives finely chopped
100g / 4oz of mushrooms very finely chopped

Serve if desired with natural soya yoghurt or tamari soya sauce (or both mixed together) over the top of the folded pancakes.

Asparagus Omelette

Serves 2
175g / 1⅓ cups of gram flour
1 teaspoon of mixed herbs
dashes of salt and pepper

Weigh out the flour and add the herbs, salt and pepper. Gradually mix in 320ml / 1⅓ cups of water, smoothing out any lumps. Set aside.

2 tablespoons of olive oil
225g / ½ lb of asparagus spears (trim off any hard end parts and slice each spear into 5 pieces)
1 medium red onion sliced into slim wedges

Sauté the vegetables in the oil, at just under medium heat, in a large non-stick frying pan, until ⅔ cooked. Then scatter the ingredients evenly around the pan and distribute the gram mixture so that it covers them and the pan base. Cook until the underneath of the mixture is just set; you may need to move the pan around the heat somewhat to ensure even cooking. Then place the omelette still in the frying pan under the grill and cook until the top is just set, otherwise it will harden.

Serve with spicy chutney or soya sauce, plus a red and green salad.

Sprouted Lentil Sauté

Sprouted lentils are highly nutritious, taste very pleasant and look nice too.

Serves 2
100g / ¾ cup of dried Puy lentils or French style lentils
(they look dark in the packet but come out blue-green)
colander
fabric serviette

Soak the lentils overnight (*see recipe Sprouted Wheat Berry Breakfast on page 144 for the sprouting method*).

225g / ½lb of pasta shapes
1 tablespoon of olive oil
150g / 1¹/₃ cups of purple topped turnips cut into slivers
2 tomatoes chopped
4 to 5 spring onions / scallions chopped, including
green parts
a few dandelion leaves or parsley chopped, discard stems
1 tablespoon of tamari soya sauce
1 tablespoon of cider vinegar
1 tablespoon of vegetable fat spread
salt and pepper to taste

Warm 2 plates. Half fill a large pan with water and bring to boil. Meanwhile prepare the vegetables. When the water has boiled add the pasta and turn to simmer. When the pasta is 5 minutes away from fully cooked continue as below.

Sauté the turnips in the oil, in a large non-stick frying pan for a couple of minutes, then add the sprouts and sauté for 1 minute longer. Add the tomatoes, spring onions / scallions, dandelion leaves, tamari and cider vinegar and sauté for 1 minute more tossing all well in together. Then leave on a low heat.

Drain the pasta, add the vegetable fat plus salt and pepper and mix in. Divide the pasta between the 2 plates; top with the lentils and vegetables, including any juice.

Sprouted Wheat Berry Sauté with Pine Nuts

Serves 2
125g / ¾ cup of whole wheat grains
colander
fabric serviette

Soak the grains overnight (*see recipe Sprouted Wheat Berry Breakfast on page 144 for the sprouting method*).

1 tablespoon of olive oil
50g / ⅓ cup of pine nuts
6 spring onions / scallions including any decent green parts chopped
10 radishes cut in half
a few dandelion or lettuce leaves chopped
2 tomatoes chopped
juice of half a lemon
½ tablespoon of shoyu soya sauce
salt and pepper to taste

Warm 2 plates. Sauté the pinenuts in the oil, in a large non-stick frying pan, for 3 minutes, then add the sprouted wheat grains and spring onions / scallions and sauté 2 minutes longer.

Finally add the rest of the ingredients mixing well in.

Easy Lasagne

Nutritious and delicious.

Serves 2
1 large onion finely chopped
200g / ½lb of spinach finely chopped
230g can / ¾ cup of tomatoes chopped
1 teaspoon of mixed herbs
2 tablespoons of tamari soya sauce
100g / 4oz of mushrooms finely sliced
salt
12 sheets of ready cooked lasagne
12 tablespoons of natural soya yoghurt
8 to 10 tablespoons of ground almonds

Steam the onion and spinach for 4 minutes. Drain and set aside with the lid off.

Mix the tomatoes, herbs, tamari, 100ml / ½ cup of water, mushrooms and dashes of salt together in a bowl to make a sauce.

Distribute 6 of the sheets of lasagne into the bottom of 2 oven dishes, so that each one has 3 overlapping sheets. Spread the onion and spinach evenly over the top followed by the yoghurt. Top with the remaining lasagne overlapping as before. Immediately spoon on the sauce, covering the sheets completely.

Sprinkle evenly with the ground almonds taking care to cover the edges of the pasta.

Bake immediately (otherwise the pasta curls) at gas 5 / 375°F for 30 minutes, turning the dishes halfway through the cooking time

Pizza

Serves 4 to 6
300g / 2¼ cups of strong whole wheat flour
dashes of salt
1 teaspoon of commercial bread yeast powder e.g.
Fermipan

Mix the above together with 250ml / 1⅛ cups of water. Knead for a couple of minutes and then make into a ball. Roll out on a floured surface, turning a few times during the process, until approximately 8mm / ⅓ inch thick. Then fold in half, place over the rolling pin and transfer to a large, greased, non-stick oven tray (preferably a round pizza tray) then unfold.

> 2 medium onions chopped in half and sliced into fine semi-circles
> 200g can / ¾ cup of pitted black olives cut in half
> (reserve 100ml / ½ cup of the brine in a measuring jug)
> 150g / 6oz of mushrooms sliced
> 280g / 1¾ cups of tofu cubed
> 2 tablespoons of tamari soya sauce
> 1 tablespoon of olive oil
> 1 tablespoon of oregano or marjoram
> 100g / ½ cup of tomato puree

Arrange first the onions, then the olives and mushrooms and finally the tofu over the dough.

Add the tamari, oil, herb and tomato puree to the reserved brine, plus enough water to make up to 350ml / 1½ cups and mix all well in together. Spoon this mixture evenly over the pizza making sure the tofu is coated.

Leave to rise for a couple of hours to double its bulk. Bake at gas 5½ / 385ºF for 30 minutes, turning halfway through the cooking time.

Serve with baked or new potatoes and a green salad if desired.

Smoked Tofu with Ginger in Sweet & Sour Sauce

Serves 4

2 tablespoons of sesame oil
2 handfuls of walnuts broken
2 medium carrots finely sliced
small head of white cabbage finely sliced
2 medium red onions sliced into slim wedges
1 tablespoon of root ginger finely chopped
300g / 2 cups of smoked tofu cubed
400 ml / 1⅔ cups of apple juice
1¼ tablespoons of corn flour
3 tablespoons of shoyu soya sauce

Warm 4 plates.

Sauté the walnuts, carrots and cabbage in the oil, in a large non-stick frying pan, until nearly tender. Then add the onions, ginger and tofu and cook until all tender (adding a little water if the mixture becomes too dry).

Pour in the apple juice. Blend the corn flour with the shoyu and add mixing in well. Gradually bring to boil stirring constantly. Then simmer for 3 minutes stirring regularly.

Serve at the side of whole grains or noodles with extra shoyu if wished.

Oriental Savoury Noodles

Serves 2
1 tablespoon of sesame oil
1 large carrot cut into thick matchsticks
2 handfuls of cashew nuts
2 or 3 dried shiitake mushrooms cut into bits, discard
the stems
a few strands of hijiki or arame sea vegetable
225g / ½ lb of noodles
½ tablespoon of finely chopped root ginger
225g / ½ lb of bean sprouts
bunch of spring onions / scallions or 1 leek chopped,
include any decent green parts
tamari soya sauce

Warm 2 plates.

Sauté the carrot, leek (if used) and cashews in the oil, in a large non-stick frying pan, until the vegetables are half tender, then turn the heat very low.

Half fill a large pan with water and add the shiitake and sea vegetable. Bring to boil, add the noodles and simmer, loosening them as they cook.

Whilst the noodles are cooking return to the sautéing. Turn the heat up again, add the ginger and cook for 2 minutes, then add the bean sprouts and cook for a further 2 minutes; finally add the spring onions / scallions (if used) and cook for 1 minute longer, then keep warm on lowest heat.

When the noodles are cooked, drain, reserving any left over stock. Place them on the plates and cover with the vegetables, adding a generous sprinkling of tamari plus a little of the stock water if wished.

Spinach Florentine Style

Try this for a pleasing way with spinach.

Serves 2
2 tablespoons of rapeseed oil
1 large onion chopped
225g / ½ lb of spinach or Swiss chard chopped
(discard any stem ends)
sprinkling of salt
280g / 1¾ cups of tofu cubed
1 or 2 teaspoons of made up mustard
1 tablespoon of shoyu soya sauce
¼ mug / ⅓ cup of soya milk
small packet of ground almonds

Sauté the onion in the oil, in a large non-stick frying pan, for a couple of minutes. Then add the spinach or chard plus salt and sauté until the vegetables are tender. Place the cooked ingredients at the bottom of a large oven dish.

Put the tofu, mustard, shoyu and soya milk in a flat-bottomed dish and mash with the back of a fork. Spread the mixture over the vegetables and then sprinkle generously with the ground almonds.

Bake at gas 4 / 350°F for 25 minutes turning the dish halfway through the cooking time.

Serve with new potatoes and grated carrot if wished.

Spanish Omelette

Make the same gram flour mixture as in the recipe for asparagus omelette (*see page 51*).

Serves 2
2 tablespoons of olive oil
1 large potato diced very small
1 small red bell pepper (discard the top then de-seed and slice into thin strips)
1 small onion finely chopped

Sauté the vegetables in the oil, at just under medium heat, in a large non-stick frying pan, until the potato is tender. Then complete the omelette as in the asparagus recipe.

Tomato & Mushroom Omelette

Make the same gram flour mixture as in the recipe for asparagus omelette (*see page 51*).

Serves 2
2 tablespoons of olive oil
1 small onion finely chopped
100g / ¼ lb of mushrooms sliced
7 baby tomatoes chopped

Sauté the onion and mushrooms in the oil, at just under medium heat, in a large non-stick frying pan, until ²/₃ cooked. Add the tomatoes. Then complete the omelette as in the asparagus recipe.

Broccoli
with Pasta & Spicy Sauce

Serves 2
Spicy Nut Butter Sauce: see under Sauces for the recipe
225g / ½lb of ribbon pasta
1 medium carrot finely sliced
2 small heads of broccoli or 1 smallish cauliflower cut
into florets (discard most of the stem)
1 tablespoon of rapeseed oil
salt

Warm 2 plates. Make the nut butter sauce and set aside; re-heat when the pasta is nearly tender, add a little water if the sauce becomes too thick.

Half fill a large pan with water and bring to boil, add the pasta, carrot and broccoli or cauliflower, then turn to simmer. Loosen the ribbons as soon as they begin to soften and cook until tender.

Drain the pasta and vegetables and place on a low heat. Add the oil and a sprinkling of salt, tossing all well in.

Place the ribbon pasta and vegetables on the plates and pour the re-heated sauce over the top.

Chapattis
with Celery, Apples, Walnuts
& Creamy Tarragon Sauce

Serves 3
olive oil
3 large sticks of celery finely sliced
75g / ¾ cup of walnuts broken
1 medium onion chopped
2 medium red apples
salt and pepper
6 whole wheat chapattis

Place 1 tablespoon of olive oil in a large non-stick frying pan. Add the celery, walnuts and onion and sauté until two thirds tender. Then chop and add the apples, plus a sprinkling of salt and pepper. Sauté until the vegetables are just tender.

Grease a non-stick roasting tin. Divide the above mixture equally between the chapattis, filling one side and folding the other side over and place in the tin. Coat the top of each one with a little olive oil and sprinkle with water. Bake at gas 4 / 350°F for 20 minutes, turning the tin halfway through the cooking time.

4 tablespoons of whole wheat flour
2 teaspoons of tarragon
1 tablespoon of barley miso
300ml 1¼ cups of soya milk
1 teaspoon of cider vinegar

Place the first 3 ingredients in a pan and gradually add the milk, mixing to a creamy consistency. Then add 300ml / 1¼ cups of stock or water and place on a high heat, stirring constantly until the sauce thickens. Then turn to simmer for a couple of minutes, adding the vinegar plus salt and pepper to taste and mixing in.

Serve the chapattis with the sauce and a green and red salad if you wish.

Spicy Gram Pancakes

2 large or 4 small servings
1 tablespoon of rapeseed oil
2 medium red onions sliced into slim wedges
4 large sticks of celery finely sliced
8 tablespoons of commercial spicy chutney
8 tablespoons of natural soya yoghurt
shoyu soya sauce

Sauté the onions and celery in the oil, in a large non-stick frying pan until ¾ cooked. Take off the heat and mix in the chutney; set aside.

> 100g / ¾ cup of strong whole wheat flour
> 100g / ¾ cup of gram flour
> sprinkling of salt

Weigh out the flours and add the salt and gradually mix in 500ml / 2¼ cups of water, smoothing out any lumps. Then cook the pancakes as in the recipe on page 132.

Immediately after starting the final pancake, finish cooking the vegetables. When all the pancakes are cooked, open, fill with the vegetable mixture and the yoghurt, then fold in half again. Serve sprinkled with the shoyu.

Basmati & Pine Nut Stuffed Peppers with Creamy Tomato Sauce

Serves 4

2 medium onions finely chopped
400g / 2 cups of basmati whole grain rice
50g / ⅓ cup of pine nuts
3 tablespoons of raisins
1 teaspoon each of rosemary and thyme
2 tablespoons of olive oil
dashes of salt

1 tablespoon of shoyu soya sauce
4 large green bell peppers (remove the tops and seeds and discard)
750ml / 3 cups of tomato juice
180g / ¾ cup of natural soya yoghurt
small bunch of parsley chopped, discard stems

Place all the ingredients in the first section in a large pan and sauté for 3 minutes mixing all well in. Place 1 litre / 4 cups of water over the mixture. Bring to boil and simmer gently on the lowest heat with the lid on, until all the water is absorbed (about 30 minutes). Then lift the lid and only now add the shoyu mixing well in.

Stuff the peppers with the rice mixture pressing it well down inside them. Place the leftover rice at the bottom of a large greased casserole dish with 120ml / ½ cup of water. Put the peppers upright on top and cover with the lid.

Bake at gas 6 / 400°F for 30 minutes turning the dish halfway through the cooking time.

When the peppers have only 5 minutes left to cook place the tomato juice, yoghurt and parsley in a pan and bring to a gentle simmer stirring occasionally; add salt if required. Place a pepper and ¼ of the extra rice on each plate and top with the sauce.

Bulgar, Avocado & Pecan Salad

Serves 2 as a main meal
200g / 1⅓ cups of bulgar wheat
4 spring onions / scallions including green parts,
chopped
3 medium tomatoes chopped small
1 small bunch of parsley chopped (discard ends)
100g / ¾ cup of cucumber chopped small
2 tablespoons of olive oil
2 tablespoons of cider vinegar
1 garlic clove crushed
salt and pepper to taste
1 large ripe avocado (not too soft)
1 small packet of pecans

Place the bulgar in a large pan with 2½ times its volume of water. Bring to boil and place the lid on. Then simmer gently until the water is absorbed (approximately 15 to 20 minutes).

Meanwhile prepare the spring onions / scallions, tomatoes, parsley and cucumber.

Mix the oil, vinegar, garlic, salt and pepper together in a dish.

When the bulgar is cool add the vegetables and dressing, mixing all well in together. Place onto dinner plates.

Halve the avocado and scoop out the flesh making about 7 'little shells' per half using a teaspoon. Arrange the shells side by side in the centre of the salad sprinkling them with a little cider vinegar and salt. Place a pecan in the centre of each shell.

Golden Pizza

2 large or 4 small servings
large commercial whole wheat pizza base
280g / 1¾ cups of tofu cubed
120ml / ½ cup of soya milk
5 tablespoons of ground almonds
1 tablespoon of tamari soya sauce
sprinkling of salt and pepper
1 small onion very finely chopped

Place the base in a greased non-stick pizza tray. Put the tofu, milk, almonds, tamari and salt and pepper in a flat-bottomed dish and mash with the back of a fork. Then mix in the onion. Place the mixture over the pizza base covering right up to the edges. Bake at gas 5 / 425°F for 20 minutes turning halfway through the cooking time.

1 tablespoon of olive oil
small green bell pepper (discard the top then de-seed and slice into thin strips) or 100g / ¼lb of mushrooms sliced
6 pieces of sun dried tomato soaked for 10 minutes and cut up finely
a few baby tomatoes chopped
½ teaspoon of rosemary

When the base has only 5 minutes left to cook sauté the pepper or mushrooms in the oil in a non-stick frying pan for 3 minutes. Then add the tomatoes and rosemary and sauté 2 minutes longer. Cut the cooked base into portions and top with the vegetables.

Serve with new potatoes and salad if desired.

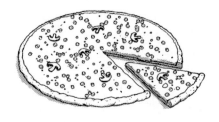

Millet, Sweet Corn & Cashew Salad

Serves 2 as a main meal
200g / 1 cup of millet
50g / ½ cup of broken cashew nuts
1 teaspoon of olive oil
4 spring onions / scallions including green parts chopped
1 bunch of watercress chopped
½ bunch of radishes (or equivalent baby purple topped turnips) chopped
2 large tomatoes chopped small
baby can / 1 cup of sweet corn drained
1 tablespoon of olive oil
2 tablespoons of cider vinegar
salt and pepper to taste

Place the millet in a large pan with 2½ times its volume of water. Bring to boil, then simmer gently with the lid on until all the water is absorbed (approximately 15 to 20 minutes).

Meanwhile sauté the cashews in a pan with 1 teaspoon of oil and a sprinkling of salt, until lightly browned.

Prepare the spring onions / scallions, watercress, radishes and tomatoes and place in a dish along with the sweet corn.

When the millet has cooled, loosen it using your fingers if necessary. Add the cashews and vegetables along with the oil, vinegar, salt and pepper and toss all well in.

Pasta, Olive & Bean Salad

Serves 2 as a main meal

225g / ½lb of pasta shells
knob of vegetable fat spread
4 spring onions / scallions including green parts chopped
half a bunch of radishes or equivalent baby purple topped
turnips chopped
400g can / 1½ cups of soya beans drained and rinsed
(or other beans of choice)
2 medium carrots grated
5 large cos lettuce leaves cut into strips plus a few
whole baby leaves from the centre
200g can / ¾ cup of pitted black olives drained and
chopped in half (reserve the brine)

In a large pan, cook the pasta until al dente, drain, and add the vegetable fat spread, tossing well in.

Whilst the pasta is cooking, prepare the spring onions / scallions and radishes and place in a bowl along with the beans.

Grate the carrot and keep separate. Prepare the lettuce and spread it over 2 dinner plates.

Add the chopped olives and the brine to the cooked pasta and mix in. Then add the onions, radishes and beans and stir well in.

Place over the lettuce and put the grated carrot in the centre.

Potato & Chickpea Salad

Serves 2 as a main meal
450g / 1lb of new potatoes
knob of vegetable fat spread
salt and pepper
4 spring onions / scallions including green parts chopped
100g / ¼lb of mange tout pods / snow peas
½ bunch of radishes chopped
410g can / 1⅓ cups of chickpeas drained
1 medium carrot grated
8 to 10 tablespoons of natural soya yoghurt

In a medium pan, boil the potatoes gently in their skins until tender; drain and chop into small chunks. Add the vegetable fat plus salt and pepper to taste and mix all well in together.

Whilst the potatoes are cooking prepare the spring onions / scallions, mange tout / snowpeas and radishes and place in a bowl along with the chickpeas; grate the carrot and keep separate.

Place the cooked potatoes on two plates and spread the salad and chickpeas over them, then scatter the carrot over the top. Finish by adding 4 to 5 tablespoons of soya yoghurt per plate, spreading it out in small clumps.

Serve with crusty bread if wished.

Rice & Red Bean Salad

Serves 2 as a main meal
200g / 1 cup of whole grain basmati rice
4 spring onions / scallions including green parts chopped
2 red apples chopped
75g / 4 cups of rocket / arugula
3 tablespoons of sunflower seeds
420g can / 1½ cups of red kidney beans drained
1 tablespoon of olive oil
2 tablespoons of cider vinegar
2 teaspoons of coarse wholegrain French mustard
salt and pepper to taste

Place the rice in a large pan with 500ml / 2 cups of water. Bring to boil then simmer very gently with the lid on, until the water is absorbed, about 30 minutes.

Meanwhile prepare the onions/ scallions, apples and rocket / arugula and place in a dish along with the sunflower seeds and the drained kidney beans.

When the rice has cooled add the salad, beans and seeds. Mix the oil, vinegar, mustard, salt and pepper together and add to the rice mixture, toss well in.

Spinach Frittata

Serves 4

100g / 4oz of vermicelli or other small pasta
1 tablespoon of rapeseed oil
1 large onion very finely chopped
225g / 8oz of spinach very finely chopped
2 garlics crushed
240ml / 1 cup of soya milk
400g / 2²/₃ cups of tofu cubed
2 tablespoons of barley miso or 1¹/₃ tablespoons of
yeast / vegetable extract
2 teaspoons of oregano
1 teaspoon of basil
²/₃ mug / 1 cup of ground almonds
sprinkling of salt and pepper
small packet of flaked almonds

Cook the vermicelli, drain and set aside.

Whilst the pasta is cooking sauté the onion, spinach and garlic in the oil, in a large non-stick frying pan until tender, then set aside.

Place the cooked vermicelli, soya milk, tofu, miso, oregano, basil, ground almonds, salt and pepper together in a large dish. Mash all well in together using a potato masher. Then mix in the vegetables.

Place in a 20cm / 8 inch, greased non-stick quiche dish, pressing well down and smoothing out to a dome shape. Decorate the top with enough flaked almonds to completely cover the surface, pressing down well.

Bake at gas 4 / 350ºF for 30 minutes, turning the dish halfway through the cooking time.

Do not cut or serve until cool (not chilled). If desired serve with a green and red salad and crusty bead.

Trottole with Tempeh Rashers

Quick, easy and eye-catching

Serves 2
5 tempeh rashers cooked as per the instructions on
the packet
225g / ½ lb of trottole or other spiral pasta
2 tablespoons of olive oil
2 small red onions sliced into slim wedges
a little dulse cut up small or 6 pieces of sun dried
tomato soaked for 10 minutes and cut up small
half a bunch of radishes sliced in two
small bunch of rocket / arugula, discard any stems
shoyu soya sauce
optional: small packet of ground almonds

Warm 2 plates. After cooking the rashers cut into bite sized pieces; set
aside. Cook the pasta as per the instructions on the packet.

Whilst the pasta water is heating up, sauté the onions and dulse in half
the oil, in a large non-stick frying pan until the onion is half tender.
Then add the rashers and radishes and cook 1 minute longer. Keep warm
on lowest heat until the trottole is cooked.

When the pasta is tender drain and place on a low heat. Add the sautéed
ingredients, remaining oil, rocket / arugula and dashes of shoyu and toss
all well in.

Place on the plates. If using ground almonds make a well in the centre
of each portion and fill with the ground almonds. Serve with extra shoyu
if desired.

Creamy Spinach
with Pasta Shells

Pleasing and easy to make.

Serves 2
225g / 8oz of pasta shells
200g / 1⅓ cups of tofu cubed
125g / ½ cup of natural soya yoghurt
1 tablespoon of tamari soya sauce
⅓ teaspoon of nutmeg
dashes of salt and pepper
225g / 8oz of spinach finely chopped
1 large or 2 small red onions sliced into slim wedges

Warm 2 plates. Bring to boil half a large pan of water, then add the shells and simmer until tender.

Meanwhile, mash the tofu, yoghurt, tamari, nutmeg, salt and pepper together using the back of a fork, to form a slightly lumpy mixture and set aside.

When the pasta has only 5 minutes left to cook, steam the spinach and onion together in a large pan.

When cooked, drain the shells and vegetables and place together in one pan along with the tofu mixture. Cook for 2 minutes more tossing all well in together.

Mushroom & Onion Quiche

Traditional fare with a new look

Serves 4
150g / 1¼ cups of strong whole wheat flour
dashes of salt
75g / ⅓ cup of vegetable fat spread

Weigh out the flour and add the salt and fat, mixing together using your fingers, until breadcrumb like. Add 80ml / ⅓ cup of water and knead the mixture lightly into a dough. Roll out on a floured surface, turning a few times during the process. Then transfer to a 20cm / 8 inch, non-stick quiche dish.

2 tablespoons of rapeseed oil
1 large onion finely chopped
150g / 6oz of mushrooms sliced
400g / 2⅔ cups of tofu cubed
120ml / ½ cup of soya milk
3 tablespoons of strong whole wheat flour
2 tablespoons of barley miso or 1⅓ tablespoons of yeast / vegetable extract
2 teaspoons of mixed herbs

Sauté the onion and mushrooms in the oil, in a large non-stick frying pan, until the onion is nearly cooked.

Mash the tofu, milk, flour, miso and herbs in a flat bottomed dish using a potato masher.

Combine the onion and mushrooms with the tofu mixture and place in the pastry case pressing well down. Bake at gas 5 / 375ºF for 35 minutes, turning the dish halfway through the cooking time.

Serve if wished with new potatoes plus a red and green salad.

Polenta with Florence Fennel

Serves 4
2 tablespoons of tamari soya sauce
250g / 1 ½ cups of polenta
75g / ¾ cup of ground almonds
dashes of salt and pepper

Fill a large pan with water equal to 4 times the volume of the polenta. Add the tamari and bring to boil. Meanwhile place the polenta, ground almonds, salt and pepper in a bowl and mix together.

When the water has boiled turn to simmer. Add the polenta mixture to the pan in fistfuls, allowing it to stream through your fingers, stirring constantly. Then simmer for 4 minutes more, stirring regularly.

Place the mixture into a large greased non-stick roasting tin and leave to cool. Then bake at gas 5 / 375°F for 30 minutes, turning the tin halfway through the cooking time.

1 tablespoon of olive oil
1 Florence fennel thinly sliced (discard leaves and
2½ cm / 1 inch of the base)
2 medium red onions sliced into slim wedges
1 teaspoon of basil
8 tablespoons of natural soya yoghurt

When the polenta is half cooked, sauté the fennel in the oil, in a large non-stick frying pan for 7 minutes. Then add the onions and basil and sauté until all tender, about 7 minutes more. Add a few tablespoons of water whilst sautéing to stop the vegetables drying out.

Cut the polenta into 4 portions and serve topped with the vegetables and yoghurt. If wished serve with a leafy green salad.

Spaghetti Napolitana

Serves 4
2 tablespoons of olive oil
2 large onions chopped
500g / 1lb of spaghetti
2 garlic cloves crushed
225g / ½ lb of mushrooms sliced
2 medium sized carrots grated
400g can / 1¾ cups of premium tomatoes chopped
400g can / 1½ cups of pitted black olives drained,
reserve 100ml / ½ cup of the brine
50g / ¼ cup tomato puree
½ tablespoon each of oregano and thyme
1½ tablespoons of tamari soya sauce
100g / 1 cup of ground almonds
bunch of parsley chopped (discard stems)

Put 4 plates to warm. Sauté the onions in the oil, in a medium sized pan until nearly tender, set aside.

Cook the spaghetti in a large pan, as per the instructions on the packet. Drain, add a splash of olive oil and toss together using 2 forks. Divide up between the 4 plates.

Whilst the pasta water is heating add the garlic and mushrooms to the onions and cook until all tender.

Then add the carrots, tomatoes, olives, brine, tomato puree, 100ml / ½ cup of water, the herbs and tamari. Bring to boil mixing all well in together and simmer until the sauce thickens a little. Then keep warm on lowest heat until the spaghetti is cooked; add a little water if the sauce becomes too thick.

Serve the sauce on top of the spaghetti. Make a well in the centre of each serving and fill with ground almonds. Garnish with parsley.

Avocado Sauce
with Ribbon Pasta

Serves 2
1 tablespoon of olive oil
1 large onion chopped fine
1 garlic clove crushed
225g / ½lb of ribbon pasta
1 medium sized ripe avocado
1 large carrot grated
200g can / ¾ cup of pitted black olives drained and cut
in half (reserve 125ml / ½ cup of the brine)
⅓ mug / ½ cup of soya milk
1 tablespoon of tamari soya sauce
½ teaspoon of deep red paprika
bunch of watercress chopped (discard ends)

Warm 2 plates.

Sauté the onion and garlic in the oil in a pan, until half tender, set aside.

Cook the pasta in a large pan until al dente.

While the ribbon pasta is cooking mash the avocado in a small dish using the back of a fork; add to the onion and garlic along with the carrot, olives, retained brine, milk, ⅓ mug / ½ cup of water, tamari and paprika. Bring to boil and simmer for a few minutes stirring from time to time.

Divide the pasta between the 2 plates, place the sauce over it and garnish with the watercress.

Cream of Lettuce & Peas

This simple dish is easy to make and very enjoyable.

Serves 2
225g / 8oz of pasta bows
250g / 1¾ cups of frozen petite pois
250g / 1 cup of natural soya yoghurt
1 teaspoon of tarragon
sprinkling of salt and pepper
1 tablespoon of olive oil
2 small red onions sliced into slim wedges
8-10 large deep green cos lettuce leaves sliced into
thick strips

Warm 2 plates. Half fill a large pan with water and bring to boil. Add the bows and simmer until 2 minutes away from tender, then add the peas.

Whilst the pasta water is heating place the yoghurt, tarragon, salt and pepper in a dish and mix together. Set aside.

Sauté the onions in the oil in a large non-stick frying pan, until half cooked. Keep on a low heat until the peas are added to the pasta, then turn the heat up again and add the lettuce to the onions and sauté for 1 minute. Remove the pan from the heat.

When cooked, drain the pasta and return the pan to a low heat. Add the yoghurt mixture, onions and lettuce, tossing all well in together.

Fresh Broad Beans / Fava Beans with Pasta Bows

Serves 2

1kg / 2¼lb of unshelled broad beans / fava beans, shelled
225g / ½lb of pasta bows
2 tablespoons of olive oil
2 tablespoons of cider vinegar
½ teaspoon each of rosemary and mint
dashes of salt and pepper
200g can / ¾ cup of pitted black olives drained and halved (reserve the brine)
2 large tomatoes chopped small
optional: small bunch of parsley chopped (stalks discarded)

Put 2 plates to warm. Shell the broad beans / fava beans.

Bring half a large pan of water to boil, then add the pasta and broad beans / fava beans and simmer.

Whilst the bows and beans are cooking place the oil, vinegar, rosemary, mint, salt, pepper, olives, brine and tomatoes plus the parsley if used, all together in a dish.

When the pasta is cooked, drain and add the rest of the ingredients, mixing all well in using 2 large serving spoons.

Garden Peas & Pasta

Fresh garden peas are a treat to look forward to.

Serves 2
25g / ⅓ cup of sun dried tomatoes chopped small
650g / 1½lb of unshelled peas shelled
1 tablespoon of olive oil
1 large red onion sliced into slim wedges
100g / ¼lb of mushrooms sliced
225g / ½lb of pasta bows or shells
salt and pepper to taste
6 tablespoons of ground almonds
small bunch of fresh parsley or mint chopped (discard stems)

Put 2 dinner plates to warm. Soak the tomatoes for 30 minutes in just enough hot water to cover them. Shell the peas.

Place half a large pan of water on to boil. Meanwhile put the oil in a large non-stick frying pan and sauté the onion until half cooked, then add the mushrooms and cook until all tender, set aside.

When the water is boiling add the peas and pasta to it, reduce to simmer and cook until the pasta is tender, then drain. Place back on the heat and add the tomatoes plus ¼ mug / ⅓ cup of their soaking water, the onions and mushrooms, salt and pepper to taste and the ground almonds; mix all well in.

Place on the plates and garnish with the parsley or mint.

Green Bean, Zucchini & Smoked Tofu Crumble

Serves 2

1 tablespoon of rapeseed oil
1 large onion chopped
150g / 6oz of French beans / green beans sliced
2 small courgettes / zucchini sliced
150g / 1¼ cups of smoked tofu cubed
230g can / 1 cup of premium tomatoes chopped
1 tablespoon of barley miso or 2 teaspoons of yeast /
vegetable extract
1 teaspoon each of basil and oregano
4 tablespoons of natural soya yoghurt

Sauté the onion, beans, courgettes / zucchini and cubed tofu in the oil, in a large non-stick frying pan, until just tender. Add the tomatoes, miso, 250ml / 1 cup of water, herbs and yoghurt mixing all well in together. Simmer for 2 minutes and then place in a large oven dish.

75g / ¾ cup of oat flakes (not whole or jumbo oats)
6 tablespoons of strong whole wheat flour
dashes of salt
4 tablespoons of vegetable fat spread

Mix all the above together using your fingers, until breadcrumb like. Sprinkle over the other ingredients. Bake at gas 5 / 375°F for 25 minutes, turning the dish halfway through the cooking time.

Moulded Summer Medley

Here is something a little different from the usual salad.

Serves 4
8 radishes chopped
4 spring onions / scallions including green parts chopped
small bunch of parsley chopped (discard stems)
2 medium carrots grated
1 tablespoon of nori flakes
2 410g cans / 2²/₃ cups of red kidney beans drained
500ml / 2¼ cups of apple juice
1 tablespoon of shoyu soya sauce
1 tablespoon of Gelozone (or use another unflavoured
vegan thickener like Agar Agar, following the instructions
on the packet)

Prepare the vegetables and place in a bowl along with the nori flakes and beans. Mix all well in together. Distribute the mixture between 4 bowls pressing well down.

Place the apple juice and shoyu into a medium pan and sprinkle evenly with the Gelozone and mix in. Bring to boil stirring constantly. Take off the heat as soon as it bubbles, then pour equally over each of the bowls and leave to set; refrigerate if wished.

Serving suggestion: Carefully loosen the moulds with a knife and tip them onto 4 plates. Encircle with chopped salad leaves, radishes and new potatoes. Top the moulds with a little natural soya yoghurt if desired.

Summer Stew

Full of earthy flavours.

> **Serves 4**
> 900g / 2lb of new potatoes
> salt
> knob of vegetable fat spread
> 1kg / 2¼ lb of unshelled broad beans / fava beans shelled
> 2 tablespoons of olive oil
> 3 to 4 new season carrots chopped
> 2 large onions chopped
> 400g / 1lb of runner beans / string beans chopped
> 3 medium courgettes / zucchini sliced
> 1 teaspoon each of rosemary and mint
> 1½ tablespoons of barley miso or 1 tablespoon of
> yeast / vegetable extract
> 2 tablespoons of cider vinegar
> 50g / ¼ cup of tomato puree
> *optional*: small packet of ground almonds
> crusty bread

Boil the potatoes gently in their skins, in a large pan, until tender. Drain, chop into chunks and add a sprinkling of salt. Mix in the knob of vegetable fat spread. Divide equally between 4 dinner plates and set aside.

Put the oil in a large non-stick frying pan and sauté the carrots for 3 minutes, then add the onions and sauté for 3 minutes longer.

Transfer the sautéed vegetables to a large pan and add the broad beans / fava beans, runners / string beans, courgettes / zucchini, rosemary, mint, miso, vinegar and tomato puree and mix all well in together using 2 serving spoons. Add 350ml / 1½ cups of water and bring to boil, then simmer strongly with the lid on until the vegetables are just tender, approximately 10 minutes.

Whilst the above is cooking pop the plates of potatoes into the oven and warm through for 10 minutes at gas 3 / 325°F.

When all is cooked, stir the stew and place over the potatoes. Serve topped with ground almonds and crusty bread.

Sweet & Sour Summer Noodles

A lovely way with summer vegetables

Serves 2
1 tablespoon of corn flour
1⅓ tablespoons of rice miso
1 teaspoon of finely chopped root ginger
300ml / 1¼ cups of apple juice

Place the flour, miso and ginger in a pan and gradually add the apple juice, mixing all well in together as you do so. Bring to boil stirring constantly then remove from the heat and set aside.

200g / 7oz of 5 minute noodles
1 tablespoon of sesame oil
2 small red onions sliced into slim wedges
1 medium courgette / zucchini sliced
1 large corn cob husked; remove the corn from the cob
100g / 4oz of mange tout / snow peas
150g / 6oz of bean sprouts

Cook the noodles. Whilst the noodle water is heating up sauté the onions and courgette in the oil, in a large non-stick frying pan, until half tender. Add the corn and mange tout / snow peas and cook until all are just tender. Then add the beansprouts and sauce and sauté 1 minute longer. Leave on lowest heat until the noodles are tender.

Drain the cooked noodles and add to the rest of the ingredients. Turn the heat up again and cook 1 minute longer tossing all well in together using 2 serving spoons.

Tofu-Nut Truffles

Eat on the hoof or as part of a meal.

Serves 4
280g / 1¾ cups of tofu cubed
⅔ mug / 1 cup of ground almonds
⅔ mug / 1 cup of crispy malted wheat flakes crushed
between your fingers (or use a similar cereal product)
125g / ½ cup of vegan mayonnaise
juice of half a lemon
dashes of salt and pepper
2 tablespoons of shoyu soya sauce
small packet of chopped hazelnuts
optional: light sprinkling of paprika or cayenne pepper
and/or 1 teaspoon of dried chives or nori flakes

Place all the above (except the hazelnuts) together in a flat bottomed dish, along with 60ml / ¼ cup of water. Mash all well in together with the back of a fork; then form into 16 balls. Sprinkle some of the chopped hazels on to a plate and gently cover the balls with them.

Serve as part of a salad meal if desired.

Zucchini Pizza

Serves 4 to 6
300g / 2¼ cups of strong whole wheat flour
1 teaspoon of commercial bread yeast powder
e.g. Fermipan
dashes of salt

Mix the above together with 275ml / 1⅛ cups of water. Knead the dough for a couple of minutes and then make into a ball. Roll out onto a floured surface, turning a few times during the process, until approximately 8mm / ⅓ inch thick. Then fold in half, place over a rolling pin and transfer to a large, greased, non-stick oven tray (preferably a round pizza tray) then unfold.

> 3 medium courgettes / zucchini cut into 12mm / ½ inch thick rounds
> 150g / 6oz of mushrooms sliced
> 1 large onion chopped in half and sliced into fine semi circles
> 230g can / 1 cup of tomatoes chopped
> 2 tablespoons of olive oil
> 1 teaspoon each of basil and oregano
> salt
> 8 tablespoons of ground almonds

Lay the courgettes / zucchini over the pizza base followed by the mushrooms and top with the onion. Place the tomatoes in a bowl and mix in the oil, herbs and 80ml / 1⅓ cup of water. Spoon this mixture over the whole of the pizza, sprinkle with salt and the ground almonds.

Leave to rise for a couple of hours to double its bulk. Bake at gas 5½ / 385ºF for 30 minutes, turning the tray halfway through the cooking time.

Serve with new potatoes and green salad if wished.

Cauliflower au Gratin

An old favourite brought up to date.

Serves 4
1 large cauliflower cut into florets (discard most of the stem)
2 large onions chopped

Steam the florets and onions until the cauliflower is tender. Then place the vegetables in a greased non-stick roasting tin.

Make the Creamy Savoury Sauce (*see page 36*) and pour over the vegetables and bake at gas 5 / 400°F for 25 minutes, turning the tin halfway through the cooking time.

Serve if wished with a salad of rocket / arugula, diced red apples, chopped celery and wholegrain basmati rice.

Moussaka Vegan Style

The lentil sauce in this recipe is particularly enjoyable.

Serves 4
250g / 1⅓ cups of dried lentils (not red)
3 bay leaves
1 tablespoon of marjoram or oregano
1 teaspoon of cinnamon
2 or 3 garlic cloves crushed
1½ tablespoons of barley miso
400g can / 1¾ cups of premium tomatoes chopped
3 medium courgettes / zucchini cut into 12mm / ½in slices
2 large onions chopped
3 tablespoons of olive oil
2 medium aubergines / eggplants cut into 12mm / ½in slices
500g / 2 cups of natural soya yoghurt
small packet of ground almonds
small bunch of parsley chopped, stems discarded
baking foil

Cook the lentils with the bay leaves in a large pan, until the pulses are tender, keeping the water level just above them; do not drain. Aim for a 'condensed soup' consistency when cooked. Then add the marjoram or oregano, cinnamon, garlic, miso and tomatoes, bring to boil and simmer for a couple of minutes stirring all well in.

Whilst cooking the lentils place the courgettes / zucchini and onions in a non-stick roasting tin and toss in half of the oil. Spread the aubergine / eggplant slices out on a chopping board, brush one side with the rest of the oil and sprinkle with salt. Place the slices in with the rest of the vegetables and mix all well in together with 2 serving spoons.

Cover the roasting tin with foil and bake at gas 5 / 375°F for 30 minutes, turning the tin halfway through the cooking time. When ready open the foil away from yourself as the vegetables will be steaming hot.

Pour the cooked lentil mixture over the vegetables. Spoon the yoghurt over the top smoothing out with the back of the spoon, then sprinkle with the ground almonds. Pop back into the oven without the foil and bake at gas 5 / 375°F for 30 minutes, turning halfway through the cooking time.

Garnish with the parsley and serve with crusty bread if desired.

N.B. As an alternative to the courgettes / zucchini, 2 medium bell peppers (any colour) can be used. Discard tops and de-seed, then cut them into strips and toss in oil as before.

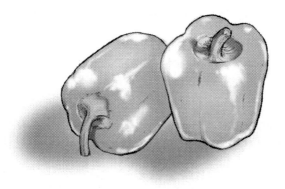

Baked Courgettes or Pumpkins with Savoury Rice

Serves 4
2 large onions chopped
400g / 2 cups of short grain whole rice
80g / 1 cup of pecans
2 tablespoon of raisins
2 teaspoons of mixed herbs
2 tablespoons of olive oil
dashes of salt
400g can / 1¾ cups of premium tomatoes chopped
3 tablespoons of shoyu soya sauce (add only after the rice is cooked, otherwise it will harden it)
1200g / 2½lb of courgettes / zucchini sliced in half lengthways or 1 small pumpkin seeded and quartered
olive oil
small bunch of parsley chopped, ends discarded

Place the first 7 ingredients in a large pan and sauté for 3 minutes mixing all well in.

Place the tomatoes and 750ml / 3 cups of water over the mixture. Bring to boil then simmer very gently on the lowest heat with the lid on, until all the liquid is absorbed (about 35 minutes). Then lift the lid and add the shoyu stirring well in.

Whilst the rice is cooking coat 4 oven dishes with the oil and place the courgettes / zucchini or pumpkins cut side up therein. Brush the tops with the oil and sprinkle with salt. Bake at gas 7 / 425°F for 30 minutes or until tender, turning the dishes and swapping shelves halfway through the cooking time.

When the rice is cooked spoon it over the cooked courgettes or pumpkins and garnish with the parsley.

Note: Pumpkin seeds can be roasted on a greased non-stick oven tray. Spread the seeds out on the tray and sprinkle with tamari soya sauce or salt. Bake at gas 7 / 425°F for 20 minutes, turning halfway through the cooking time.

You can also dry fry pumpkin seeds until they 'pop' then season as above.

Baked Summer/Autumn Vegetables with Hijiki & Pecans

The sea vegetable in this dish permeates the vegetables pleasantly.

Serves 4
a few strands of hijiki or arame sea vegetable
2 large onions chopped
3 medium courgettes / zucchini chopped chunky
500g / 1lb 4oz of runner beans / string beans sliced
2 medium carrots chopped
2 corn cobs husked, remove the corn from the cobs
2 tablespoons of sesame oil
280g / 1¾ cups of tofu cubed
100g / 1 cup of pecans
tamari soya sauce
baking foil

Place the sea vegetable in a pan with 400ml / 1¾ cups of water, bring to boil and simmer with the lid on for 15 minutes.

Meanwhile, prepare the vegetables and place in a non-stick roasting tin. Add the cooked hijiki and 100ml / ½ cup of its cooking water, or if none is left use water. Then add the oil and mix all well in together using 2 serving spoons.

Scatter the tofu and pecans all over the top of the vegetables, then liberally sprinkle with tamari.

Place the foil over the roasting tin, sealing down around the edges. Bake for 45 minutes at gas 7 / 425°F turning the tin halfway through the cooking time.

Open the foil away from yourself as the bake will be steaming hot. Serve with basmati whole grain rice and extra tamari if wished.

Autumn Stir Fry

Serves 2
20 fresh chestnuts
325g / 11oz of Brussels sprouts (trim off the very end and
peel off the 2 outer leaves) cut in half if they are large
200g / 1 cup of whole short grain rice
1 tablespoon of sesame oil
1 large red onion sliced into slim wedges
1 teaspoon of thyme
1 large red apple
150ml / ²/₃ cup of apple juice
1 tablespoon of corn flour
2 tablespoons of tamari soya sauce
1 or 2 sheets of sushi nori cut to make tiny food wraps

Cut a cross in the chestnuts and simmer in enough water to cover, until
the cross opens (about 20 minutes). Then leave to stand in cold water.

Steam the sprouts in a large pan until just tender, drain, and tip into a
bowl.

Rinse the pan and use it to cook the rice in 500ml / 2¹/₈ cups of water
with dashes of salt, bring to boil and then simmer very gently with the
lid on for 30 minutes.

Meanwhile take the chestnuts out of the water one at a time and shell.
Then cut each one into 2 or 3 pieces.

Sauté the onion and chestnuts along with the thyme in the oil, in a large
non-stick frying pan, until the onion is nearly cooked. Chop the apple
and add along with the sprouts and sauté until the onion becomes
tender. Then add the apple juice plus 125ml / ½ cup of water. Blend
the corn flour with the tamari in a mug and add to the pan mixing well
in. Gradually bring to boil stirring constantly; then simmer for 2 minutes
seasoning with salt to taste. Do not let the sauce dry out, add a little
more water if it does.

Serve with the rice. Make little food parcels with the nori as you eat.

Chestnut Crumble

Tuck into this on a November night.

Serves 2
18 fresh chestnuts
1 tablespoon of rapeseed oil
1 medium leek including any decent green parts sliced
up small
2 medium red apples
1 tablespoon of rice miso or 2 teaspoons of yeast /
vegetable extract
1 teaspoon of thyme
dashes of pepper
1 tablespoon of whole wheat flour
250ml / 1 cup of soya milk

Cut a cross in the chestnuts and simmer in just enough water to cover, until the cross opens (about 20 minutes), then leave to stand in cold water. When cooled take out of the water one at a time and shell. Then cut them in half.

Sauté the chestnuts and leek in the oil, in a large non-stick frying pan, until the leek is nearly tender. Chop and add the apples and sauté 2 minutes longer. Then add the miso, thyme and pepper and sprinkle in the flour mixing all together.

Add the milk and 250ml / 1 cup of water. Cook at a little under medium heat stirring constantly until the sauce thickens slightly, then place in a large oven dish.

75g / ¾ cup of oatflakes (not jumbo or whole oats)
6 tablespoons of strong whole wheat flour
dashes of salt
4 tablespoons of vegetable fat spread

Mix all the above together using your fingers, until breadcrumb like. Sprinkle over the other ingredients. Bake at gas 5 / 375°F for 25 minutes, turning the dish halfway through the cooking time.

Potatoes & Chestnuts au Gratin

Serves 4
vegetable fat spread
1300g / 3lb of potatoes cut into thin rounds
2 large onions chopped small
200g / ½lb of vacuum packed chestnuts sliced into 3
200g / ½lb of chestnut mushrooms sliced
200g / ½lb of ground almonds
salt and pepper
deep red paprika
500ml / 2 cups of soya milk
baking foil

Grease a non-stick roasting tin and place one third of the potatoes therein. Cover with one third of the onions, one third of the chestnuts and mushrooms, and sprinkle with 5 tablespoons of ground almonds plus salt and pepper. Repeat this process twice more, and then sprinkle paprika over the top.

Gently pour the milk plus 250ml / 1 cup of water from a jug into a corner of the tin. Cover with baking foil sealing down well around the edges.

Bake at gas 7 / 425°F for 50 minutes turning the tin halfway through the cooking time. Then remove the foil (away from yourself to prevent scalding).

Serve with a green vegetable if desired.

Roasted Artichokes
& Brussels Sprouts

Serves 4
450g / 1lb of Jerusalem artichokes scrubbed but not
peeled, chopped into small chunks
2 large red onions sliced into slim wedges
600g / 1¼lb of sprouts, trim the ends and remove the
outermost leaves
2 large carrots chopped into chunks
3 tablespoons of sesame oil
salt
baking foil

Place the vegetables in a non-stick roasting tin with the oil, sprinkle
with salt and toss all well in together. Place the foil over the tin,
sealing down around the edges and cook in the oven at gas 7 / 425°F
for 20 minutes. Then remove the foil away from yourself to avoid the
hot steam, turn the tin and cook for a further 20 minutes.

Serve with a creamy sauce and whole grains if wished.

Aduki & Parsnip Pie

Serves 4
250g / 1¼ cups of dried adukis soaked overnight
optional: 9cm / 3½ inch strip of kombu cut up small

Cook the pulses in the soaking water in a large pan, with the sea vegetable (if used) until tender. Keep the liquid just above the pulses until nearly cooked, then allow the water to dwindle, do not drain.

> 4 medium parsnips chopped into small chunks
> 1kg / 2¼lb of potatoes chopped into medium chunks
> salt and pepper to taste
> 2 large leeks including any decent green parts, chopped small
> 2 tablespoons of olive oil
> 2 or 3 garlic cloves crushed
> 1½ tablespoons of barley miso or 1 tablespoon of yeast / vegetable extract
> 4 tablespoons of tomato puree
> 1 tablespoon of cider vinegar
> vegetable fat spread

Whilst the adukis are cooking place the parsnips and potatoes in a large pan with enough water to just cover them, bring to a boil and simmer rapidly until tender, about 10 minutes.

Drain the stock into a jug and mash the vegetables, adding salt and pepper and enough stock to make into a light creamy texture; set aside.

Sauté the leeks in the oil, in a large non-stick frying pan and when half cooked add the crushed garlic and continue sautéing until the leeks are tender; set aside.

When the beans are fully cooked add the miso, tomato puree, cider vinegar and 250ml / 1 cup of the vegetable stock, simmer for a couple of minutes mixing all well in, then stir in the leeks.

Place the mixture in a greased non-stick roasting tin. Top with the mash and smooth out with the back of a fork. Spread vegetable fat over the top of the mash with the back of a fork. Bake at gas 5 / 375ºF for 30 minutes, turning the tin halfway through the cooking time.

Bavarian Bean & Cabbage Dish

A nourishing and warming meal.

Serves 4
225g / 1½ cups of dried red kidney beans soaked
overnight with 1 teaspoon of clove heads (leave these in,
once cooked the cloves will soften completely)

The next day cook in the soaking liquid in a large pan, until tender,
keeping the water level just above the beans, do not drain.

2 large red onions sliced into slim wedges
medium sized, purple tinged winter cabbage or Savoy
chopped (choose one with good green outer leaves)
2 large red apples
250ml / 1 cup of apple juice
1½ tablespoons of barley miso or 1 tablespoon of
yeast / vegetable extract

100g / ⅓ cup of tomato puree
2 or 3 garlic cloves crushed
1 tablespoon of corn flour

Steam the onions and cabbage in a large pan until just tender, drain off
any stock into a jug and set the vegetables aside with the lid off.

When the beans are tender, chop and add the apples. Then add the
apple juice, miso, tomato puree and garlic. Bring to boil and simmer for
a couple of minutes, stirring all well in.

Put the corn flour in a mug and blend with 3 tablespoons of water,
pour over the bean mixture, stirring in. Then add the cooked cabbage
and onions and mix in. Simmer for 3 more minutes stirring from time
to time.

Serve with whole grains or baked potatoes if desired.

Brussels Sprouts
& Walnut Crumble

Super supper dish.

Serves 2
350g / 12oz of small sprouts (trim the ends and
remove the outermost leaves)
1 tablespoon of rapeseed oil
1 large red onion chopped
50g / ½ cup of walnuts broken
2 medium red apples chopped
1 teaspoon of thyme
250ml / 1 cup of apple juice
1 tablespoon of rice miso
1 tablespoon of corn flour

Steam the sprouts in a large pan until just tender, drain and place in
a bowl.

Sauté the onion in the oil, in a large non-stick frying pan, until half tender.
Then add the walnuts and apples and sauté until the onion is tender.
Add the sprouts, thyme, apple juice and miso. Blend the flour with 3
tablespoons of water and add. Gradually bring to boil stirring constantly.
Then place in a large oven dish.

75g / ¾ cup of oatflakes (not jumbo or whole oats)
6 tablespoons of strong whole wheat flour
dashes of salt
4 tablespoons of vegetable fat spread

Mix all the above together using your fingers, until breadcrumb like.
Sprinkle over the other ingredients. Bake at gas 5 / 375°F for 25 minutes,
turning the dish halfway through the cooking time.

Bubble & Squeak

Make this up to the end of February only as after then the spuds tend to become too watery.

Serves 4
4 medium parsnips chopped into small chunks
2 large carrots chopped into small chunks
800g / 1¾lb of potatoes chopped into medium chunks
2 large leeks finely chopped
small bunch of cabbage greens finely chopped
salt and pepper to taste
vegetable fat spread

Steam the first 3 ingredients in a large pan until tender. Steam the leeks and cabbage greens in a separate large pan for 5 minutes.

Drain off any left over liquid from all the above into a jug. Mash the parsnips, carrots and potatoes adding salt and pepper to taste; do not add any leftover liquid as the mixture should be quite stiff. Then mix in the leeks and greens.

Turn into a greased non-stick roasting tin and press down. Spread vegetable fat over the top with the back of a fork. Bake at gas 8 / 450°F for 30 minutes turning the tin halfway through the cooking time.

Serve along with a bean dish.

Butterbeans in Brown Sauce

This will give you a boost on the coldest of days

Serves 4
250g / 1⅓ cups of dried butterbeans
9cm / 3½ inch strip of kombu cut up small

Cook the above in a large pan until tender; keeping the water level just above the beans, do not drain.

1 large onion chopped
1 tablespoon of rapeseed oil
1 tablespoon of barley miso
optional: 1 tablespoon of corn flour

Sauté the onion in the oil until tender. Add to the beans when they are cooked along with the miso. Simmer for a couple of minutes stirring well.

If the sauce is not thick enough put the corn flour in a mug and blend with 2 tablespoons of water; add this to the sauce and simmer 2 minutes more, stirring well.

Serve with hot pot vegetables or bubble and squeak if wished.

Butterbean Stew

Serves 4
250g / 1⅓ cups of dried butterbeans
optional: 9cm / 3½ inch strip of wakame (or 1 or 2
strands) cut up small

Cook the above in a large pan until tender, keeping the water level just above the beans, do not drain.

> 1 small swede / rutabaga
> 2 large carrots
> 4 large potatoes
> 2 large onions or 2 medium leeks
> (the above 4 ingredients chopped into small chunks)
> large bunch of kale leaves or cabbage greens or sprout tops, chopped
> 2 tablespoons of barley miso or 1½ tablespoons of yeast / vegetable extract
> 1½ teaspoons each of marjoram and thyme
> salt and pepper

Place the swede / rutabaga and carrots in a large pan with just enough water to cover, bring to boil then simmer briskly for 4 minutes. Then add the potatoes, keeping the water level just above the ingredients and cook until all are tender. Add the onions or leeks plus the greens mixing well in and simmer 2 minutes longer, but do not add any more water. Turn off the heat and leave the lid off

When the legumes are tender add them to the vegetables along with their cooking liquid plus the miso and herbs. Bring to boil then simmer for a couple of minutes, adding salt and pepper to taste and mixing all well in.

Croutons or dumplings, along with commercial brown sauce can be served with this stew if desired.

Cottage Pie with Gravy

A fine strong dish for a wintry day.

> **Serves 4**
> 250g / 1⅓ cups of dried lentils (not red)
> *optional*: 9cm / 3½ inch strip of wakame (or 1 or 2
> strands) cut up small

Cook the lentils and sea vegetable (if used) in a large pan until tender. Keep the water level just above the pulses, do not drain.

> 1200g / 2lb 10oz of potatoes cut into chunks
> dashes of salt and pepper
> 2 medium carrots chopped
> 2 medium leeks chopped (if there is not much green
> on the leeks add a few chopped cabbage greens)
> 1 teaspoon each of marjoram and thyme

Cook the potatoes in a large pan with just enough water to cover, this won't take long. Then drain the stock off into a jug, add salt and pepper to taste and keep adding back the stock as you mash the potatoes, until they are quite creamy.

When the lentils are tender mix in the carrots, leeks and herbs and bring to boil, but do not add any more water. Place the lid on and simmer until tender (approximately 8 minutes).

Spread the mixture over the bottom of a non-stick roasting tin, cover with the mash and smooth out with the back of a fork.

Pop in the oven and cook for 30 minutes at gas 5 / 375°F, turning the tin halfway through the cooking time.

Whilst the pie is cooking make the gravy (*see page 42*).

Dumplings or Dinner Bites

150g / 6oz of whole wheat bread
150g / 1⅛ cups of strong whole wheat flour
dashes of salt
1 teaspoon of bicarbonate of soda
optional: herbs; small onion chopped fine and sautéed;
a few mushrooms chopped fine and sautéed;
1 tablespoon of tamari soya sauce

Dumplings
Break the bread into small pieces, add 100ml / ½ cup of water and mash into a stiff dough with the back of a fork, placing the index finger in the centre of the forks head as you do so. Add the flour, salt and bicarb plus approximately 50ml / ¼ cup of water and mix into a stiff dough using your fingers. Now add any of the optional ingredients if desired and fold in thoroughly.

Fill a large pan one third full of water and bring to boil. Make the dough into 20 firm balls by rolling between your palms, and drop 10 of these one at a time into the water as it boils. Turn the heat down and simmer for 10 minutes. Using a slotted spoon, remove the dumplings onto a plate. Then bring the water back to boil and repeat the process for the other 10.

Serve in soups or stews by placing the cooked dumplings in the pot for the last 5 minutes cooking time of the soup or stew.

Dinner Bites
Any left over dumplings can be cut into bite sized chunks and fried in sesame oil with a chopped onion. Sprinkle with tamari and serve with roasted root vegetables and a whole grain if desired.

Gardener's Pie
with Lentil Sauce

This pie is very filling and sustaining.

Serves 4
medium swede / rutabaga or equivalent parsnips
chopped into small chunks
2 large carrots chopped into small chunks
2 leeks or 2 large onions chopped
large bunch of kale leaves chopped
4 medium sized potatoes sliced into 12mm / ½ inch
thick rounds
dashes of salt

Place all the ingredients except the potatoes and salt in a non-stick roasting tin and mix together. Pour 150ml / ⅔ cup of water over them. Cover with the potato rounds and sprinkle with salt.

300g / 2¼ cups of strong whole wheat flour
dashes of salt
150g / ¾ cup of vegetable fat spread

Mix the above together using your fingers until like rough breadcrumbs. Then add 100ml / ½ cup of water and knead lightly and quickly into a dough. Roll out on a lightly floured surface, turning occasionally until as big as the roasting tin. Fold in half and unfold over the tin. Cut any excess dough away from the sides of the tin with a knife (so that the edge of the dough rests on the rim of the tin) and crimp the edges by pinching between two fingers. Cut slits into the top to let out the steam. Bake at gas 5 / 375°F for 1 hour turning the tin halfway through the cooking time.

Meanwhile make the Lentil Sauce (*see page 39*).

When the pie is cooked cut the pastry into 4 pieces and lay on kitchen paper. Dish out the filling onto 4 plates, top with the sauce, and cover with the pastry.

Hot Pot with Tempeh in Sweet & Sour Sauce

Deeply satisfying.

Serves 2
9cm / 3½ inch strip of kombu cut up small
350g / ¾lb of swede / rutabaga sliced into 5mm / ¼ inch thick rounds
2 large potatoes sliced into 12mm / ½ inch rounds
2 medium red onions sliced into slim wedges
1 tablespoon of sesame oil
227g / ½lb of tempeh or seitan cut into bite sized pieces
salt
small bunch of kale leaves chopped

Place the sea vegetable at the bottom of a large pan. Then add first the swede / rutabaga, next the potatoes and finally the onions all in individual layers. Add 150ml / ¾ cup of water and bring to boil, then turn to simmer and place the lid on, do not stir. Whilst the above is cooking, sauté the tempeh or seitan in the oil, in a large non-stick frying pan, for a few minutes, sprinkling with salt. Then add to the hot pot along with the kale, but do not mix in.

1 tablespoon of corn flour
1 tablespoon of rice miso or 2 teaspoons of yeast / vegetable extract
300ml / 1¼ cups of apple juice

Finally, start making the sauce by placing the corn flour and miso into a pan and gradually adding the apple juice, mixing in as you do so. Test the swede and potato with a knife to see if they are tender and if so place the sauce on the heat and bring to boil stirring constantly. Then turn to simmer for half a minute stirring to prevent sticking.

Dish the hot pot out and pour the sauce over it.

Irish Stew with Dumplings

A traditional recipe with a new slant.

Serves 4
200g / 1½ cups of whole wheat self-raising flour
dashes of salt and pepper
100g / ½ cup of vegetable fat spread

Mix all the above together using your fingers, until breadcrumb like. Add 100ml / ½ cup of water and knead lightly and quickly into a dough. Make into 16 dumplings and place on a greased non-stick oven tray; set aside.

100g / 1⅓ cups of textured soya protein
2 tablespoons of rapeseed oil
2 large carrots chopped
2 large onions chopped
3 tablespoons of tamari soya sauce
700g / 1lb 10oz of potatoes diced
large bunch of cabbage greens chopped
230g can / 1 cup of tomatoes chopped
1½ teaspoons of sea vegetable granules, e.g. wild wrack
or 1 tablespoon of nori flakes
salt to taste

Soak the soya protein in plenty of water for 5 minutes, then drain.

Place the oil in a large non-stick frying pan and sauté the carrots, onions and soya protein for 5 minutes. Then add the tamari and mix in. Set aside.

Place the potatoes, cabbage, sautéed ingredients, tomatoes and sea vegetable in a large pan and mix together. Add 1½ litres / 6½ cups of water and bring to boil. Then simmer strongly until just tender, seasoning with salt to taste and stirring occasionally to prevent sticking.

Whilst the stew water is boiling up, bake the dumplings at gas 5 / 375ºF for 15 minutes, turning halfway through the cooking time. Keep warm until the stew is nearly cooked; then submerge the dumplings in the stew and cook for 5 minutes longer.

Nishime Style Hot Pot

A hearty oriental dish.

Serves 4
9cm / 3½ inch strip of wakame (or 1 or 2 strands) cut
up small
1 small to medium celeriac cut into 5mm / ¼ inch
rounds (if rounds are very large, cut in half) or 1 bunch
of celery chopped small
3 large parsnips or equivalent swede / rutabaga cut into
5mm / ¼ inch thick rounds
2 large carrots cut as above
2 tablespoons of sesame oil
300g / 10oz of tempeh or seitan cut into bite sized pieces
1 tablespoon of finely chopped root ginger (if wished)
2 tablespoons of corn flour
4 tablespoons of shoyu soya sauce

Place the sea vegetable at the bottom of a large pan. Then add first the
celeriac or celery, next the parsnips or swede / rutabaga and then the
carrots all in individual layers. Add 500ml / 2 cups of water and bring to
boil, then turn to simmer and place the lid on, do not stir the ingredients.

Whilst the above is cooking, sauté the tempeh or seitan with the ginger
(if used) in the oil, in a large non-stick frying pan, until lightly browned;
then place on the top of the stewing vegetables and cook until all are
tender, which won't take long.

Mix the corn flour and shoyu together in a large bowl. Drain the stock
from the cooked vegetables into the bowl (this should be about 500ml /
2 cups, if not add water) and mix in. Return all to the pan, bring to boil,
then turn to simmer for 1 minute, do not stir.

Serve with whole grains or Udon noodles.

Pea, Leek & Potato Pie with Creamy Nori Sauce

A robust meal to keep you going for many hours.

Serves 4
275g / 1¾ cups of dried yellow split peas

Cook the above in a large pan until tender, keeping the water level just above the peas until nearly cooked; then let the water dwindle, do not drain.

> 3 medium leeks chopped small including any decent green parts
> 1 kg / 2lb of potatoes cut into large chunks
> 4 large parsnips cut into small chunks
> salt and pepper to taste
> 2 tablespoons of shoyu soya sauce

Whilst the peas are cooking steam the leeks in large pan until just tender, then transfer to a dish and set aside.

Cook the potatoes and parsnips in the pan used for the leeks, with just enough water to cover. Bring to boil and simmer until tender, about 10 or 12 minutes. Then drain the stock into a jug and mash the vegetables, adding salt and pepper to taste and enough of the stock to make a light creamy texture, set aside.

Mix the cooked peas, leeks and the shoyu together and place in a greased non-stick roasting tin. Place the mash in a layer on top, and smooth out with the back of a fork.

Bake at gas 5 / 375°F for 30 minutes, turning the tin halfway through the cooking time.

Meanwhile make the Creamy Nori Sauce (*see page 41*). When the pie is ready, pour the sauce into a jug, for everyone to help themselves.

Roasted Root Vegetables

Serves 4
1 medium swede / rutabaga
2 large parsnips
2 large carrots
2 large onions or 2 medium leeks
(all the above chopped into small chunks)
3 tablespoons of rapeseed oil
salt
baking foil

Place the vegetables in a non-stick roasting tin with the oil, sprinkle with salt and toss all well in together. Place the foil over the tin, sealing down around the edges and cook in the oven at gas 7 / 425°F for 25 minutes. Then remove the foil away from yourself to avoid the hot steam, turn the tin and cook for a further 20 minutes.

Serve as an accompaniment to another dish.

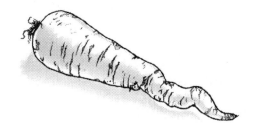

Yorkshire Pudding with Vegan Sausages

Serves 4 to 6
2 tablespoons of olive oil
250g / 1¾ cups of strong whole wheat flour
dashes of salt
1 teaspoon of bicarbonate of soda
5 commercial vegan sausages (pre cooked and chopped small)

Grease a non-stick, 12 place, deep bun tray with the oil and pop it in the oven at gas 8 / 450°F for 10 minutes.

Meanwhile place the flour, salt and bicarb in a bowl and gradually add 500ml / 2 cups of water stirring well in. Then add the sausage pieces mixing in thoroughly.

Spoon the mixture into the pre-heated tray (keeping it at arms length in case of splash back from the hot fat) and turn the oven to gas 7 / 425°F. Cook for 30 minutes turning the tin halfway through the cooking time.

Can be served with roast potatoes or parsnips plus Brussels sprouts, and gravy.

Any left over puddings can be sprinkled with water and reheated for 20 minutes at gas 5 / 375°F if wished.

Baked Gnocchi
with Mushroom Sauce

Serves 4 to 6
500ml / 2 cups of soya milk
3 tablespoons of shoyu soya sauce
200g / 1⅓ cups of semolina
salt and pepper
small packet of ground almonds

Place 800ml / 3⅓ cups of water in a large pan along with the milk and shoyu and bring to boil.

Whilst the above is heating up weigh out the semolina into a bowl and season liberally with salt and pepper.

When the liquid has boiled turn to simmer. Add the semolina to the pan in fistfuls allowing it to stream through your fingers, stirring constantly (the last dregs of the semolina can be poured in slowly from the bowl). Then carry on simmering the mixture for 2 minutes stirring constantly.

Place the mixture into a greased non-stick roasting tin or large pizza tray and top with the ground almonds, then allow to cool.

Bake at gas 5 / 375°F for 30 minutes turning the tin halfway through the cooking time.

Make the Mushroom Sauce (*see page 37*) and pour it over each portion after they have been placed onto dinner plates.

Serve with roast potatoes and a green vegetable if desired.

Boston Baked Beans

A popular favourite.

Serves 4
250g / 1⅓ cups of dried cannellini beans soaked
overnight
optional: 9cm / 3½ inch strip of wakame (or use 1 or 2
strands) cut up small

The next day cook the beans in their soaking liquid along with the sea
vegetable (if used) in a large pan, until tender, keeping the water just
above the beans. When cooked drain the liquid into a measuring jug
and return 300ml / 1¼ cups to the pan (if less than 300ml / 1¼ cups
available then make up with water)

100g / ½ cup of tomato puree
2 garlic cloves crushed
1 tablespoon of barley miso or 2 teaspoons of
yeast / vegetable extract
1 or 2 teaspoons of strong chilli sauce
1 tablespoon of cider vinegar
salt to taste

Add all the above except the salt to the pan and bring to boil, then turn
to simmer for 2 minutes, mixing all well in. Season with the salt. Place
in an open topped casserole and bake at gas 5 / 375°F for 30 minutes,
turning the casserole halfway through the cooking time. Add a little hot
water if the beans start to dry out.

Serve with mashed potatoes and vegetables if desired.

N.B. You could double the above recipe and store any not eaten; cover,
place in the fridge and use within 3 days.

Chapattis
with Butterbean Filling

Serves 2
1 tablespoon of olive oil
1 large onion chopped
12 large kale leaves chopped
420g can / 1½ cups of butterbeans drained
2 teaspoons of barley miso or yeast / vegetable extract
4 tablespoons of natural soya yoghurt
4 to 6 whole wheat chapattis
1 large carrot grated

Sauté the onion and kale in the oil, in a large non-stick frying pan, until tender, then set aside.

Place the butterbeans, miso and yoghurt in a flat bottomed dish. Mash all well in together with the back of a fork, placing the index finger in the centre of the fork head as you do so. Put the mashed ingredients in with the cooked vegetables and stir well in together.

Lay out 4 to 6 chapattis and fill one side with the mixture and fold the other side over. Place in 2 greased oven dishes, sprinkle with water and bake at gas 4 / 350°F for 20 minutes, turning the dishes halfway through the cooking time.

Whilst the food is cooking grate the carrot and then sprinkle over the chapattis just before serving.

Chapattis
with Leek & Mushroom Filling

Serves 2
1 tablespoon of olive oil
2 medium leeks including any decent green parts,
finely sliced
200g / ½lb of mushrooms finely sliced
1 tablespoon of barley miso
500g / 2 cups of natural soya yoghurt
4 to 6 whole wheat chapattis

Sauté the leeks in the oil, in a large non-stick frying pan, until ²/₃ cooked,
then add the mushrooms and miso and sauté until all tender.

Turn off the heat and mix in 6 tablespoons of the yoghurt.

Lay out 4 to 6 chapattis and fill one side with the mixture and fold the
other side over. Place in 2 greased oven dishes, sprinkle with water and
bake at gas 4 / 350°F for 20 minutes, turning the dishes halfway through
the cooking time.

Just before serving place a large blob of yoghurt over the top of each
chapatti.

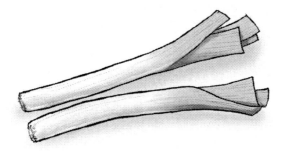

Chapattis
with Red Bean Filling

Serves 2
1 tablespoon of sesame oil
1 large onion chopped
12 large green cabbage leaves chopped
420g can / 1$\frac{1}{3}$ cups of red kidney beans drained
1 teaspoon of olive oil
2 teaspoons of barley miso or yeast / vegetable extract
2 teaspoons of chilli sauce
1 tablespoon of tomato puree
4 to 6 whole wheat chapattis
vegetable fat spread
small packet of ground almonds

Sauté the onion and greens in the sesame oil, in a large non-stick frying pan, until tender, then set aside.

Place the kidney beans, olive oil, barley miso, chilli sauce and tomato puree in a flat bottomed dish. Mash all well in together with the back of a fork, placing the index finger in the centre of the fork head as you do so. Place the mashed ingredients in with the cooked vegetables, add 3 tablespoons of water and stir well in together.

Lay out 4 to 6 chapattis and fill one side with the mixture and fold the other side over. Place in 2 greased oven dishes. Cover the top of each chapatti evenly with vegetable fat spread. Sprinkle with ground almond and bake at gas 4 / 350°F for 20 minutes, turning the dishes halfway through the cooking time.

Creamy Leek Sauté with Paprika Rice

A handy recipe for using up the leeks from the vegetable plot.

Serves 2
200g / 1 cup of whole short grain rice
dashes of salt
½ teaspoon of deep red paprika
3 large slices of medium thickness whole wheat bread,
crusts removed and coated on both sides with
vegetable fat spread
1 tablespoon of rapeseed oil
2 medium leeks finely sliced including any decent
green parts
250ml / 1 cup of soya milk
⅓ mug / ½ cup of ground almonds
½ teaspoon of ground nutmeg
salt and pepper to taste

Place the rice, salt and paprika in a large pan with 500ml / 2¼ cups of water. Bring to boil, then simmer very gently with the lid on until the water is absorbed, about 30 minutes.

Meanwhile, toast the coated bread on both sides. When cooled, crush into rough breadcrumbs using your fingers and set aside.

Put 2 plates to warm. In a large non-stick frying pan, sauté the leeks in the oil until tender. Then add the soya milk, ground almonds, nutmeg, salt and pepper and mix well in. As soon as the sauce thickens (do not let the sauce dry out, add a little more water if necessary) divide the mixture between the 2 plates filling one half of each. Sprinkle with the breadcrumbs and spoon the rice onto the other half of the plate, serve.

Note: If wished, a few chopped mushrooms can be added to the leeks halfway through their cooking time.

Crispy Italian Kale Lasagne

Serves 4
2 large onions chopped
500g / 1lb 4oz of Italian kale or ordinary kale chopped,
discard stems
2 tablespoons of vegetable fat spread
24 sheets of ready cooked lasagne
250ml / 1 cup of stock or water
500ml / 2 cups of soya milk
150g / 1½ cups of ground almonds
salt and pepper

Steam the onions and kale in a large pan until tender and drain any leftover liquid into a jug. Add the vegetable fat to the vegetables and mix well in, set aside with the lid off.

Distribute 12 of the sheets of lasagne straight from the packet onto the bottom of 4 oven dishes, so that each one has 3 overlapping sheets. Spread the kale and onions evenly over the top.

Lay the remaining 12 sheets out side by side on a clean draining board. Fill a kettle full of water and boil, then gradually pour over the pasta on the draining board until the water is used up, making sure to cover all the sheets.

When the lasagne has cooled a little place the remaining sheets on top of the vegetables, overlapping them. Pour the stock and soya milk over the pasta, sharing equally between all 4 dishes (soak all the top layers of lasagne as you pour).

Sprinkle the ground almonds over the pasta making sure you cover the sheets completely. Season with salt and pepper and bake immediately (otherwise the pasta curls) at gas 5 / 375°F for 30 minutes, turning the dishes and swapping shelves halfway through the cooking time.

Fruity Chickpea Curry

Filling and satisfying.

Serves 4
400g / 2 cups of whole grain basmati rice
salt
3 tablespoons of rapeseed oil
350g / 12oz of potatoes diced small
2 large red onions sliced into slim wedges
large bunch of kale leaves chopped
2 cloves of garlic crushed
2 medium sized red apples
3 tablespoons of raisins
2 tablespoons of korma spice blend
1½ tablespoons of barley miso
75g / ⅓ cup of tomato puree
2 400g cans / 2½ cups of chickpeas drained
jar of mango chutney

Place the rice and a sprinkling of salt in a large pan with 1 litre / 4¼ cups of water, bring to boil then simmer very gently with the lid on until all the water is absorbed (about 30 minutes).

Meanwhile in a large non-stick frying pan sauté the potatoes in the oil until nearly tender. Add the onions and cook until these are half done. Then add the kale, garlic and 150ml / ⅔ cup of water, and sauté until the kale is half tender.

Chop the apples and add them along with the raisins and curry powder, cook for 2 minutes longer. Then add 500ml / 2 cups of water, the miso, tomato puree and chickpeas, mixing all well in with a large serving spoon. When the sauce has thickened, add salt to taste if wished. Do not let the sauce dry out; add more water if necessary.

Serve on the rice, accompanied by the chutney.

Hazelnut Loaf

Serves 4
2 tablespoons of rapeseed oil
75g / ⅔ cup of commercially chopped hazels
large onion finely chopped
50g / ⅓ cup of sunflower seeds
6 large slices of medium thickness whole wheat bread,
roughly broken up
3 tablespoons of tamari soya sauce
1 tablespoon of mixed herbs or nori flakes
4 tablespoons of strong whole wheat flour
1 large carrot, grated

Sauté the hazels along with the onion and seeds in the oil, in a large non-stick frying pan, until the onion is half cooked.

Place the bread in a bowl with 125ml / ½ cup of water, the tamari and herbs or nori, and mash using the back of a fork, placing your index finger in the centre of the forks head as you do so, until dough like.

Then add the half cooked ingredients, flour and carrot and mix well in using your fingers.

Grease a 22cm / 8¾ inch, non-stick oblong bread tin and place the mixture therein. Bake at gas 5 / 375°F for 40 minutes turning the tin halfway through the cooking time.

Serve if wished with roast potatoes and parsnips, steamed Brussels sprouts and carrots, plus gravy.

Millet Bake

Serves 4
200g / 1 cup of millet
75g / ½ cup of sunflower seeds
1½ tablespoons of barley miso
½ tablespoon of sage
1 medium leek chopped
optional: 1 teaspoon of sea vegetable granules,
e.g. wild wrack

Dry roast the millet and seeds in a large pan for 3 minutes at a little under medium heat; stir to prevent burning.

Then add the miso, sage, leek and if wished the sea granules. Pour in 750ml / 3 cups of water and bring to boil stirring all well in. Turn to lowest heat setting and place the lid on, cook until the water is absorbed about 15 to 20 minutes.

Place in a 22cm / 8¾ inch, greased non-stick oblong bread tin, pressing down well. Bake for 30 minutes at gas 5 / 375°F turning the tin halfway through the cooking time.

Serve with roast vegetables or hot pot vegetables, plus gravy if desired.

Onion & Mushroom Tart

Serves 6
300g / 2¼ cups of strong whole wheat flour
sprinkling of salt
150g / ¾ cup of vegetable fat spread

Weigh out the flour and add the salt and vegetable fat, mixing all together using your fingers, until breadcrumb like.

Add 125ml / ½ cup of water and knead the mixture lightly into a dough. Roll out on a floured surface, turning a few times during the process. Then fold in half and transfer to a large round pizza or flan tin and unfold.

2 tablespoons of olive oil
3 large onions sliced into slim wedges
200g / ½lb of mushrooms sliced
1 tablespoon of barley miso or 2 teaspoons of yeast / vegetable extract

3 tablespoons of whole wheat flour
250ml / 1 cup of soya milk
50g / ½ cup of chopped hazelnuts

Sauté the onions in the oil, in a large non-stick frying pan, until half tender. Add the mushrooms and miso and sauté for a further 5 minutes. Sprinkle with the flour and mix in, then add the soya milk and stir until it thickens.

Put the mixture on to the pastry spreading out evenly and press down lightly. Sprinkle with the nuts and bake at gas 6 / 400°F for 30 minutes, turning the tin halfway through the cooking time.

Serve with baked potatoes and salad if wished.

Red Kidney Beans with Cloves in Sweet & Sour Sauce

Spicy and warming.

Serves 4
2 tablespoons of olive oil
2 large onions chopped
large bunch of kale leaves chopped
2 large red apples chopped
2/3 teaspoon of ground cloves
2 410g cans / 2 2/3 cups of red kidney beans drained
250ml / 1 cup of apple juice
100g / 1/2 cup of tomato puree
1 tablespoon of corn flour
2 tablespoons of tamari soya sauce

Warm 4 plates.

Sauté the onions and greens in the oil, in a large non-stick frying pan. Halfway through the cooking time add the apples, cloves, kidney beans, apple juice, tomato puree and 125ml / 1/2 cup of water.

Blend the corn flour with the tamari and add mixing well in. Gradually bring to boil stirring constantly, then simmer until the onions and kale are tender stirring regularly. Add a little water if the sauce becomes too thick.

Serve at the side of whole grains or noodles if desired.

Risotto Rice & Cabbage Layers with Carrot Sauce

This recipe is sweet and appetising, belying the simplicity of the ingredients.

Serves 4
2 large onions chopped
400g / 2 cups of whole short grain rice
75g / ²/₃ cup of cashews broken
1 teaspoon each of marjoram and thyme
2 tablespoons of olive oil
dashes of salt

3 tablespoons of tamari soya sauce (only add this after the rice is cooked, otherwise it will harden it)
1 large Savoy cabbage (with plenty of good green outer leaves) chopped small
Carrot Sauce (*see page 35*)

Place all the ingredients in the first section in a large pan and sauté for 3 minutes mixing all well in.

Pour 1 litre / 4¼ cups of water over the mixture. Bring to boil and simmer very gently on the lowest heat with the lid on, until all the water is absorbed (about 35 minutes). Then lift the lid and add the tamari stirring well in.

Meanwhile, steam the cabbage until just tender. Place half the cabbage at the bottom of 4 individual oven dishes and put half the rice on top. Repeat this process once more. Bake at gas 5 / 375°F for 25 minutes, turning the dishes and swapping shelves halfway through the cooking time.

Whilst the food is cooking, make the carrot sauce and spoon hot over the top of each dish just before serving.

Tortilla & Blackeyed Bean Bake with Carrot Sauce

Something a little different.

Serves 2
150g / 1 cup of dried blackeyed beans
1 large onion chopped
100g / 4oz of kale chopped
1 teaspoon of mixed herbs
5 tablespoons of ground almonds
1 tablespoon of shoyu soya sauce
salt and pepper to taste
4 wheat flour tortillas

Cook the blackeyed beans in a large pan, keeping the water level just above the beans; when they are tender add the onion and kale and mix in. Simmer strongly until the vegetables are tender. Do not allow the ingredients to dry out; keep at a very thick consistency, adding a little water if necessary. Then add the rest of the ingredients except the tortillas, mixing well in.

Place half the mixture at the bottom of 2 oven dishes and cover each portion with a tortilla. Repeat this process once more.

1 large carrot grated
2½ tablespoons of tomato puree
1 tablespoon of corn flour
1 tablespoon of shoyu soya sauce

Whilst the beans are cooking make the sauce by placing the first 2 ingredients in a pan with 300ml / 1¼ cups of stock or water. Place the corn flour in a mug with the shoyu and blend. Add to the sauce and place on a high heat, stirring until the sauce thickens. Then pour evenly over the top of each dish and bake at gas 7 / 425°F for 20 minutes, turning the dishes halfway through the cooking time.

Winter Hot Pot Vegetables

Serves 4
medium swede / rutabaga or celeriac or equivalent
parsnips cut into small chunks
2 large carrots cut into chunks
2 leeks or 2 large onions sliced
large bunch of cabbage or kale leaves chopped
2 tablespoons of sesame oil
sprinkling of salt
4 large potatoes sliced into 12mm / ½ inch thick rounds
baking foil

Place all vegetables except the potatoes in a non-stick roasting tin; sprinkle 1 tablespoon of the oil and a little salt over them, mixing well in with a serving spoon.

Pour 125ml / ½ cup of water in at the side of the tin. Cover with the potato rounds, brush with the rest of the oil and sprinkle with salt.

Cook covered with baking foil at gas 6 / 400°F for 50 minutes turning the tin halfway through the cooking time. When cooked open the foil away from yourself to avoid the hot steam.

Serve if wished with millet bake and gravy or butterbeans in brown sauce.

Winter Noodle Sauté

Try this for something quick and satisfying

Serves 2
1 tablespoon of sesame oil
2 large sticks of celery plus a few baby celery heart
pieces chopped small
2 medium red onions sliced into slim wedges
1 mug / 1¹/₃ cups of extremely thin slices of swede /
rutabaga
1 medium leek including any decent green parts, chopped
2 teaspoons of finely chopped root ginger
225g / ½ lb of soba or Udon noodles
1 teaspoon of sea vegetable granules e.g. wild wrack or
dashes of salt and pepper
1 mug / 1¹/₃ cups of cooked beans (borlottis go nicely)
1 tablespoon of rice miso or 2 teaspoons of yeast /
vegetable extract

Prepare the vegetables. Place the oil in a large non-stick frying pan and
add the celery, onions, swede / rutabaga, leek and ginger and sauté until
nearly tender, then set aside.

Whilst the vegetables are cooking place 1 litre / 4¼ cups of water in a
large pan and bring to boil. Then add the noodles, sautéed vegetables,
sea vegetable granules, beans and miso. Simmer strongly until the
noodles are tender stirring occasionally. Eat with a fork and spoon.

Cannellini Creole Style

Serves 4
225 / 1½ cups of dried cannellini or haricot beans
soaked overnight or two 420g cans / 3 cups drained

If using dried beans, cook the next day in their soaking liquid in a large pan, until tender, keeping the water just above the beans; drain.

> 1 tablespoon of olive oil
> 4 or 5 large stalks of celery sliced thinly
> 2 large red onions sliced into slim wedges
> 300ml / 1¼ cups of apple juice
> 1 teaspoon of muscovado sugar
> ⅔ teaspoon of celery seed
> ⅓ or ½ teaspoon of cayenne pepper
> 2 tablespoons of tomato puree
> 2 tablespoons of tamari soya sauce
> 1½ tablespoons of corn flour
> salt

Sauté the celery in the oil, in a large non-stick frying pan for 2 minutes. Then add the onions and sauté until both vegetables are just tender. Add the apple juice, sugar, celery seed, cayenne and tomato puree and stir in. Blend the tamari in a bowl with the corn flour and add, mixing in. Gradually bring to boil stirring constantly. Then add the beans and simmer gently for 5 minutes mixing well in. Add salt to taste. Do not let the sauce dry out, add a little water if necessary.

Serve with a deep green leafy salad and Udon noodles or whole grains if wished.

Chilli Beans

Hot and tasty.

Serves 4
250g / 1¼ cups of dried flageolet beans
optional: 9cm / 3½ inch strip of kombu cut up small

Soak the beans overnight. The next day place the beans and their soaking liquid along with the sea vegetable (if used) in a large pan and cook until tender, keeping the water level just above the beans, do not drain.

>2 medium carrots, chopped
>2 large onions chopped
>2 bay leaves
>large bunch of cabbage greens chopped
>400g can / 1¾ cups of premium tomatoes chopped
>2 tablespoons of barley miso or 1½ tablespoons of
>yeast / vegetable extract
>2 crushed garlic cloves
>½ to 1 tablespoon of concentrated chilli sauce
>1 tablespoon of marjoram or oregano
>*optional*: small packet of ground almonds

When the beans are tender add the carrots, onions and bay leaves to the pan stirring well in, keeping the water level just above the ingredients.

When the vegetables are just tender add the greens, tomatoes, miso, garlic, chilli sauce and marjoram or oregano and mix all well in (do not add any more water)

Cook for a few minutes longer until the greens are tender, stirring from time to time.

Serve with spaghetti or whole grains and sprinkle with ground almonds if wished.

Mushroom & Nut Turnovers

Serves 4
300g / 2¼ cups of strong whole wheat flour
dashes of salt
150g / ¾ cup of vegetable fat spread

Mix the above together using your fingers until breadcrumb like. Then add 100ml / ½ cup of water and knead lightly and quickly into a dough. Roll out on a lightly floured surface, turning occasionally until a large square shape is obtained. Cut into 4 squares and then roll these out a little further if possible.

1 tablespoon of rapeseed oil
2 medium onions chopped
75g / ⅔ cup of hazelnuts with skins, crushed (see below
for crushing method) or use ready chopped ones
200g / ½lb of mushrooms sliced
½ tablespoon of mixed herbs
dashes of salt and pepper

Sauté the onions in the oil, in a large non-stick frying pan, for 2 minutes.

If using whole hazels, place the nuts on one side of a pot towel and fold the other side over them; roughly crush with a rolling pin, bringing it down lengthwise on them a few times.

Add the nuts to the pan along with the mushrooms, herbs, salt and pepper, mixing all well in. Sauté until the onions and mushrooms are cooked.

Place a quarter of the mixture on one side of each square and fold the other side over. Crimp the edges by pinching between 2 fingers. Cut 3 short slits into the folded edge of each turnover.

Place on 2 non-stick oven trays or roasting tins. Bake at gas 7 / 425°F for 30 minutes, turning trays or tins and swapping shelves halfway through the cooking time.

Serve with potatoes, greens and gravy if desired.

Sausage or Rasher Omelette

Make the same gram flour mixture as in the recipe for asparagus omelette (*see page 51*).

Serves 2
2 tablespoons of rapeseed oil
4 vegan sausages or 5 tempeh rashers
7 baby tomatoes chopped

Sauté the sausages or rashers in the oil, at just under medium heat, in a large non-stick frying pan, until tender; then chop them into small pieces. Add the tomatoes. Then complete the omelette as in the asparagus recipe.

Pancakes
Stuffed with Purple Sprouting
Broccoli, Pecans & Yoghurt

2 large or 4 small servings

400g / 14oz of purple sprouting broccoli including any
leaves; cut the spears to 8cm / 3 inches long and split
their stems to pencil width; discard any leftover stems,
chop any leaves
50g / ½ cup of pecans broken
1 large onion chopped
2 large tomatoes chopped
1 tablespoon of rapeseed oil
dashes of salt and pepper
8 tablespoons of natural soya yoghurt
shoyu soya sauce

Prepare the above and place the broccoli, pecans and onions in a large
pan with 150ml / ⅔ cup of water and set aside.

200g / 1⅓ cups of strong whole wheat flour
dashes of salt

Weigh out the flour and add the salt and gradually mix in 500ml / 2¼
cups of water, smoothing out any lumps. Use a medium non-stick cast
iron frying pan, or ¾ of a large one. Oil the pan and heat through for a
couple of minutes at a little under medium heat. Pour in a quarter of the
batter, distributing it evenly by gripping the pan handle with both hands
and tilting from side to side. Fry until the underside is slightly browned,
about 3 minutes. Then turn and do the other side which will cook
quicker. Fold the pancake in half and pop in the oven to keep warm.

Repeat this process 3 more times and immediately after starting the final
pancake place the pan of vegetables with the lid on, onto the stove. Turn
the heat to ¾ of its full strength and steam for 5 minutes, then turn the
heat down and check that the vegetables are tender. Drain and return to
the heat adding the tomatoes, rapeseed oil and a few dashes of salt and
pepper, tossing all well in.

When all the pancakes are cooked, open, fill with the vegetable mixture and spoon the yoghurt over the top, then fold the pancakes in half again. Serve sprinkled with shoyu soya sauce.

MISCELLANEOUS

Croutons

olive oil
whole wheat bread sliced
vegetable fat spread
optional: 2 crushed garlic cloves

Lightly cover a large non-stick frying pan with the oil and fill with the bread. Spread vegetable fat thinly over the top of each piece. Sauté until the underside is golden brown. Then turn and cook the second side.

If using the garlic, incorporate into the vegetable fat spread just before putting it on the bread.

When cooked allow to cool a little and then cut each slice into small squares.

Serve with soups, stews or salads.

Garlic Toasty

Serves 1
2 large slices of medium thickness whole wheat bread,
coated on all 4 sides with vegetable fat spread
1 large garlic clove crushed

Spread the garlic over one slice of the bread and cover with the other
slice. Grill / broil on both sides.

Nut Medley

From a cost and convenience point of view, buy your nuts in bulk, checking that they have a long-running sell-by date.

    2 handfuls of hazelnuts
    2 handfuls of pecans or walnuts
    2 handfuls of cashews
    1 tablespoon of shoyu soya sauce

Sauté the above together in a large non-stick frying pan (no oil necessary) until the shoyu has almost dried up. Cool, then bag.

Potato Cakes

Makes a nice supper dish.

> 300g / 11oz of left over roast, baked, boiled or mashed
> potatoes with any skins removed
> 7 tablespoons of strong whole wheat flour
> dashes of salt
> *optional*: 1 garlic clove crushed or 2 spring onions /
> scallions (including green parts) finely chopped
> sesame oil
> vegetable fat spread

If using roast, baked, or boiled potatoes mash them with the back of a fork. Then add the flour, salt and an option if required. Mix together using a fork. Make 6 balls with the dough and flatten into thin rounds.

Coat a large non-stick frying pan with just enough oil to cover. Cook the cakes at a little under medium heat until lightly browned, then turn and do the other side.

Serve topped with vegetable fat spread.

Quick & Easy Mixed Sautés

Sautés can be made at any time of the year to give a satisfying and varied meal without much effort. Here are some ingredients to choose from for your sauté.

Protein

flavoured or plain tofu, tempeh or seitan / left over beans, tins of beans especially baked beans / low fat vegan burgers or sausages / tinned braised tofu or nut loaf / mushrooms, etc.

Complex Carbohydrates

left over solid potatoes, swede (rutabaga), parsnips / wholemeal pitta (pocket), bread or sliced bread / left over whole grains, etc.

Green Vegetables

garden peas / French beans (green beans) / cabbage / kale / purple sprouting broccoli and leaves / Brussels sprouts / salad greens / oriental greens, etc.

Garnishes

tomatoes / grated carrot / red bell pepper / radishes / parsley / watercress / alfalfa sprouts / fresh chives / dulse bits, etc.

Pickles and Sauces

gherkins / onions / red cabbage / beetroot (beet) / spicy pickle / commercial brown sauce / mustard / tamari soya sauce, etc.

Choose a protein, complex carbohydrate and green vegetable ingredient plus a garnish and / or pickle or sauce from the above lists, or more than one of each if wished.

Example recipes are given below as a rough guide on how to make the sautés.

Example 1

Serves 2
Warm 2 plates. Prepare some Brussels sprouts.

Use a well-oiled, large non-stick frying pan and sauté a chopped onion for a couple of minutes. Then add some sliced mushrooms and a tin of braised tofu chopped. When the vegetables are nearly tender sprinkle with soya sauce and move them along with the tofu to the side of the pan away from the heat.

Sauté some left over mashed swede (rutabaga) in the space left and season with salt and pepper. At the same time steam the sprouts, then drain and toss in a knob of vegetable fat spread.

If sautéed bread is required, place all the cooked food onto the plates and pop in the oven on a low heat. Then coat the pan with a little oil and sauté some pitta (pocket) or other bread until light brown on both sides.

Example 2

Serves 2
Warm 2 plates. Prepare some mustard. Chop 2 tomatoes. Place some fresh or frozen garden peas in a pan with water to cover.

Cut left over boiled or baked potatoes into rounds and sauté in a well-oiled non-stick frying pan until lightly browned; turn and do the other side. Then move the potatoes to the other side of the pan away from the heat.

Cut some tinned nut loaf into rounds and sauté on both sides in the space left. Season with salt and pepper or soya sauce. At the same time cook the peas, then drain and toss in a knob of vegetable fat spread.

If toast is required place all the cooked food onto the plates and pop in the oven on a low heat.

Then make the toast and spread with vegetable margarine.

There are no hard and fast rules on how to make sautés, so throw yourself in at the deep end and have some fun trying different ones out.

Savoury Almond Toast

Serves 1 or 2
2 tablespoons of vegetable fat spread
5 tablespoons of ground almonds
salt
2 large thick slices of whole wheat bread

Place the fat, ground almonds and a sprinkling of salt in a flat-bottomed dish and mix to a thick paste with the back of a fork.

Smooth half the mixture over one side of the bread and grill to golden brown. Turn the toasts and repeat the process.

Serve with soups or cut into small squares and toss with salad.

Sesame Seed Paste
& Tomato Toasties

Serves 2
4 large slices of medium thickness whole wheat bread
jar of stone ground, dark sesame seed paste
2 medium sized tomatoes sliced
unpasteurised barley miso
vegetable fat spread

Spread the paste over the upper sides of 2 slices of the bread and cover with the tomato slices. Thinly spread the miso over the upper sides of the other 2 slices of bread and place on top of the first slices.

Now coat the upper side of each sandwich with the vegetable fat spread and grill / broil. Turn and coat the undersides of the sandwiches with the vegetable fat spread and grill / broil them also.

Sprouted Wheat Berry Breakfast

Serves 2
125g / ¾ cup of whole wheat grains (this amount will supply you with a few servings)
colander
fabric serviette

Soak the grains overnight. The next day, place the serviette in the colander so that it hangs over the sides. Put in the wheat and rinse it well morning, afternoon and night, for 3 days. Cover the colander with a plate after each rinse and store in a slightly warm place.

On the fourth day, if the sprouts are at least 9mm / ⅓in long, they are ready for use; if not, continue the above process for another day.

1 mug / 1⅓ cups of sprouts
1⅓ mugs / 2 cups of crispy malted wheat flakes
fruit of choice chopped
sprinkling of salt
1 mug / 1⅓ cups of soya milk

Divide the sprouts, flakes, fruit and salt equally between 2 large bowls and mix well in together. Add the milk, dividing equally. Serve immediately.

The rest of the sprouts will keep in the fridge for a few more days. Store in the colander with the serviette inside and a plate covering the top. Rinse once daily, they will continue to sprout slowly.

Yoghurt Cheap & Simple

Place 3 tablespoons of commercial natural soya yoghurt in a large jug or bowl. Pour onto the yoghurt 500ml / 2 cups of organic soya milk and add 2 pinches of salt. Stir well.

Leave in a warm (not hot) draught-free place such as an airing cupboard until it sets firmly; it is then ready for use.

> Approximate developing times:
> Cold and warm weather – 48 hours
> Very warm weather – 36 hours
> Hot weather – 24 hours

Do not let it over-develop otherwise it will go off. Once it is made keep the yoghurt covered with foil and refrigerate.

Time your next batch to overlap with the first so you don't run out of yoghurt, using 3 tablespoons of your first batch to start the next.

Picnic & Lunch Box Salads

Make easy take away meals with a selection of the following ingredients. Provide yourself with sandwich boxes or salad bowls with a lid, plastic cutlery and paper serviettes.

Base Ingredients

left over beans, sprouted mung beans, sprouted lentils or canned beans drained / sprouted whole wheat grains, bulgar wheat or cous cous soaked for the appropriate time in boiled water and drained, left over rice or millet / can of sweet corn drained / left over potatoes chopped / left over pasta, etc.

Green Salads

lettuce / watercress / rocket / chicory / parsley / baby spinach / chard leaves / cress / alfalfa sprouts / fresh chives / spring onions (scallions) including ends / packet of mixed salad greens./ cucumber / nori sea vegetable flakes, etc.

Red Salads

red onion / radishes / tomatoes / orange or red pepper / red cabbage / red apples / grated carrot / cooked beetroot / red chicory / red chard, etc

Nuts and Seeds

almonds / pecans / walnuts / hazel nuts / pumpkin seeds / pistachio nuts / sunflower seeds / brazil nuts / pine nuts / cashew nuts / peanuts, etc.

Salad Dressings

olive oil / cider vinegar / mustard / salt / pepper / crushed garlic / horse radish relish / soya sauce / fruit juice / natural soya yoghurt / diluted chilli sauce / paprika / herbs / vegan mayonnaise, etc

Choose your ingredients from each list, prepare them and place in your container/s along with the chosen dressing/s and toss all well in together.

Make your salad the night before if you wish, along with bread and vegetable fat spread, cover and refrigerate.

Scalloped Potatoes

Required amount of whole smallish potatoes with their
skins on
sesame oil
salt

Gently boil the potatoes until nearly tender. Drain and when cool enough
to handle cut into 15mm / ⅔ inch thick rounds.

Coat a large non-stick frying pan with the oil and cook the potatoes
therein until golden brown, sprinkling with salt. Turn and cook the
other side.

Makes a nice addition to baked beans and vegan sausages.

Seitan

Seitan (wheat protein) is strengthening, gives vitality and can be used in many recipes.

4 servings
1kg / 2lb 4oz of strong whole wheat flour
large mixing bowl

Place the flour in the bowl and add 880ml / 3²/₃ cups of warm water. Mix to a dough and then knead for 3 minutes. Boil up 1½ litres / 6¹/₃ cups of water in a kettle.

Place the bowl with the dough inside it into the sink. Gently run enough cold water into the bowl to cover the dough (always start the process with cold water). Knead the dough very gently under the water for 3 minutes, keeping it in a central ball, so that the bran and starch begin to seep out without the ball of dough disintegrating.

Throw out the water and gently fill the bowl with the boiled water and enough cold to make it hand hot (don't pour water directly on to the dough). Knead the dough as above for 3 minutes.

Again throw out the water and repeat the process once more, this time with cold water again.

By now the dough should be about ¹/₃ of its original size; if not do 2 more kneadings and rinses, the first one hand hot and then the last one must always be a cold rinse. Then squeeze out any excess water.

Half fill a large pan with water and bring to boil. Meanwhile make the seitan into balls slightly smaller than golf ball size. Place the seitan balls into the boiling water and turn to a strong simmer. Cook for about 7 minutes.

Remove with a slotted spoon, cool and cut into bite sized pieces; the seitan is now ready for use in your recipes.

See over for example recipes.

Example Recipes using Seitan.

Example 1

Serves 2

Sauté half of the seitan in a large, well-oiled, non-stick frying pan for 7 minutes, sprinkling with salt. Then add vegetables and seasonings and cook until the vegetables are tender. Serve if desired with whole grains or over noodles with tamari soya sauce.

Example 2

Serves 2

Sauté half of the Seitan in a large, well-oiled, non-stick frying pan for 7 minutes, sprinkling with salt. Then chop and add 1 large onion plus a few mushrooms and cook until the vegetables are tender. Make some light gravy (see under Sauces for the recipe). When the gravy is cooked place the Seitan and vegetables in it and set aside until the rest of the meal is ready, then re-heat. Serve if wished with roasted root vegetables and Brussels sprouts.

Browned Pot Barley

Here's a way of making barley much more interesting.

Serves 4 to 6
300g / 1½ cups of pot barley
2 tablespoons of sesame oil
2 tablespoons of shoyu soya sauce
optional: salt

Cook the barley in a large pan until tender (approximately 50 minutes) keeping the water level just above the barley, stir occasionally to prevent sticking.

When your accompanying dish is about 20 minutes from completion, place the drained barley in a large non-stick frying pan with the oil and shoyu and stir all well in.

Cook for 10 minutes at a little under medium heat without stirring, then turn the barley and cook for a further 10 minutes. Sprinkle lightly with salt during cooking if desired.

Serve as an accompaniment to another dish.

BAKED GOODS, PUDDINGS, ETC

Strong Bread Flour

Owing to the absence of eggs strong bread flour is used throughout this section as it has a superior binding power in comparison with soft flour.

Spelt Flour

If possible, when making bread use 50% of spelt flour which gives a superior colour, texture and flavour and is lower in gluten than other strong flours. A little less liquid might be required when using spelt flour. However, when making desserts, it is best to use an ordinary strong flour for its superior binding quality.

Storage of Baked Goods

Any goods not eaten soon after baking should be covered whilst still warm to prevent them drying out. This is necessary because of the low content of fats and absence of refined sugar, so they do not retain moisture as easily as commercial baked goods. Except for the sourdough bread, refrigerate after covering; keeping time is 3 days.

Herb Bread

300g / 2¼ cups of strong whole wheat flour
dashes of salt
1½ teaspoons of commercial bread yeast powder
e.g. Fermipan
1 tablespoon of mixed herbs
1 tablespoon of olive oil
1 tablespoon of paprika

Place all the above together in a bowl and mix in 250ml / 1 cup of water. Knead all well in together for a few minutes.

Grease a 22cm / 8¾ inch, non-stick, oblong bread tin and place the dough in this. Leave to rise to double its bulk (approximately 2 hours) then bake at gas 5 / 375ºF for 30 minutes, turning halfway through the cooking time.

Eat while still warm. Toast any leftover bread.

Sourdough Bread

This bread is tasty, strengthening and health giving.

Starter
First of all you need to make a starter. Place 275g / 2 cups of whole wheat strong flour, 250ml / 1 cup of water and a sprinkling of salt in a bowl and mix together. Leave in a warm draught free place such as an airing cupboard or a warm kitchen cupboard for a few days. Keep checking the mixture and when it has approximately doubled its size the starter is ready for use as follows.

Bread
Grease a 19cm / 7½ inch diameter, round, non-stick tin and set aside. Weigh out 550g / 4¼ cups of whole wheat strong flour and sprinkle with salt. Mix in the starter roughly using your fingers. Any lumpy bits will disperse during fermentation. Then add approximately 450ml / 1¾ cups of water, mix well in to produce a softish dough. Knead for a couple of minutes.

Next starter
Break off a piece of dough the size of a large apple towards your next starter and set this aside in a warm draught free place. After about 8 hours place the new starter in the fridge where it will keep for about 4 days.

Back to the bread
Knead the remaining bread dough (which should be quite moist) for a few minutes and place in the tin. Leave to rise in a warm draught free place. When after several hours the dough has more or less doubled its bulk, place in the oven at gas 3 / 325°F and bake for 1 hour, turning halfway through the cooking time.

Storage
Immediately after baking, whilst the loaf is still very hot, wrap in a clean cotton tea towel and then pop it in a plastic bag; this will steam the bread and stop it going hard.

Back to the starter
The day before making the next loaf, get the starter out of the fridge and mix in ⅔ mug / 1 cup of flour with enough water to make a soft dough.

Place in a warm draught free place for use the next day, by which time it should be around double its bulk. Then follow the above instructions to make your next new loaf.

The above may sound complicated but if you make this bread regularly you will find it easy to do. After 48 hours the bread is best if lightly toasted.

Sourdough Fruit & Nut Loaf

Make this loaf at the same time as you make the sourdough bread (see previous recipe). Split the starter into ²/₃ for the sourdough bread and ¹/₃ for the fruit and nut loaf.

> 300g / 2¼ cups of whole wheat strong flour
> ¹/₃ of the sourdough starter (see the first sourdough bread recipe)
> salt
> 1 teaspoon of cinnamon
> 50g / ¼ cup of vegetable fat spread
> 75g / ²/₃ cup of hazel nuts with skins (crushed as described below)
> 150g / 1 cup of dried fruit finely chopped
> 250ml / 1 cup of apple juice

Grease a 26cm / 10¼ inch, non-stick, oblong bread tin and set aside. Mix the flour, starter, sprinkling of salt, cinnamon and vegetable fat together, using your fingers, until it resembles small pieces of dough. Any lumpy bits will disperse during fermentation.

Place the hazels on one side of a pot towel and fold the other side over them; roughly crush them with a rolling pin by bringing it down lengthwise on them a few times.

Add the nuts, fruit and apple juice to the other ingredients, mixing together thoroughly. Knead for a couple of minutes.

Place the mixture in the tin and leave to rise in a warm draught free place such as an airing cupboard. When after several hours the dough has more or less doubled its bulk, place in the oven alongside the sourdough bread. Turn at the same time as the bread, but remove from the oven 15 minutes before the bread. For storage see the sourdough bread recipe. Best toasted after the first 48 hours.

Sourdough Granary Bread

Make the same recipe as for sourdough bread (*see page 156*) but substitute 300g / 2¼ cups of granary flour in place of 300g / 2¼ cups of the usual flour.

Tea Bread

300g / 2¼ cups of strong whole wheat flour
dashes of salt
1½ teaspoons of commercial bread yeast powder
e.g. Fermipan
100g / ¾ cup of raisins
3 slices of lemon finely chopped

Place all the above together in a bowl and add 300ml / 1¼ cups of water, blending all well in together.

Grease a 22cm / 8¾ inch, non-stick, oblong bread tin and place therein. Leave to rise to double its bulk (approximately 2 hours) then bake at gas 5 / 375ºF for 30 minutes, turning halfway through the cooking time.

Best toasted after the first 24 hours.

Almond Carrot Balls

Nice for a party piece.

> 75g / 1 cup of crispy malted wheat flakes or other
> similar cereal product
> 180ml / ¾ cup of soya milk
> 2 medium carrots grated
> 100g / 1¼ cups of ground almonds
> juice of a lemon
> 75g / ½ cup of raisins
> small packet of chopped hazelnuts

Place the flakes in a bowl along with the milk and leave to soak.

Grate the carrots and add to the softened flakes along with the almonds, lemon juice and raisins. Mix in using your fingers.

Make into 16 balls by rolling pieces of the mixture lightly between your palms. Sprinkle the chopped hazels onto a plate and gently cover the balls with them.

Serve in small dishes and eat with your fingers.

Apricot & Pecan Cake

300g / 2¼ cups of strong whole wheat flour
dashes of salt
2 teaspoons of bicarbonate of soda
100g / ½ cup of vegetable fat spread
1 teaspoon of cinnamon
150g / 1 cup of dried yellow apricots finely chopped
50g / ½ cup of pecans broken
250ml / 1 cup of apple juice

Mix the flour, salt, bicarb, vegetable fat and cinnamon all together using your fingers, until breadcrumb like. Then add the fruit, pecans and apple juice and mix well in. Place in a greased, 22cm / 8¾ inch, oblong non-stick tin and bake for 50 minutes at gas 3 / 325°F turning halfway through the cooking time.

Serve warm with commercial soya custard if wished.

Carrot Cake

Best made up to the end of February as after that time the carrots are losing their sweetness.

> 300g / 2¼ cups of strong whole wheat flour
> 2 teaspoons of bicarbonate of soda
> dashes of salt
> 2 teaspoons of cinnamon
> 100g / ¾ cup of sultanas / golden raisins
> 100g / ½ cup of vegetable fat spread
> 3 large carrots freshly grated
> 160ml / ⅔ cup of apple juice

Mix all the above together except the carrot using your fingers, until breadcrumb like. Then thoroughly blend in the carrot and apple juice.

Place in a greased, 22cm / 8¾ inch, non-stick oblong tin and bake for 1 hour at gas 3 / 325°F, turning halfway through the cooking time.

Serve warm with commercial soya custard if wished.

Chocolate & Orange Marmalade Buns

Enjoy with a cup of tea.

> 250g / 1¾ cups of strong whole wheat flour
> sprinkling of salt
> 1 tablespoon of bicarbonate of soda
> 5 tablespoons of sugar free cocoa powder
> 125g / ½ cup of Seville orange pure fruit spread
> 100g / ¾ cup of raisins
> 100g / ½ cup of vegetable fat spread
> 300ml / 1¼ cups of apple juice

Mix all the above together except the juice, using your fingers, then add the juice and mix well in.

Grease a non-stick, 12 place, deep bun tray and fill it with the mixture.

Bake at gas 3 / 325°F for 25 minutes, turning halfway through the cooking time.

Date & Ginger Cake

For lovers of ginger.

> 300g / 2¼ cups of strong whole wheat flour
> 2 teaspoons of bicarbonate of soda
> dashes of salt
> 125g / 1 cup of finely chopped dates
> 50g / ⅓ cup of root ginger finely chopped
> 100g / ½ cup of vegetable fat spread
> 250ml / 1 cup of apple juice

Mix all the above together (except the juice) using your fingers, until breadcrumb like. Add the juice and mix well in.

Place in a greased, 22cm / 8¾ inch, non-stick oblong tin and bake at gas 3 / 325°F for 50 minutes, turning halfway through the cooking time.

Serve warm with commercial soya custard if desired.

Fruit Slice

200g / 2 cups of oat flakes (not jumbo or whole oats)
200g / 1½ cups of strong whole wheat flour
1 teaspoon of bicarbonate of soda
dashes of salt
150g / ¾ cup of vegetable fat spread
250ml / 1 cup of apple juice
250g / 1¾ cups of dried dates or apricots chopped

Mix the first 5 ingredients together using your fingers until like coarse breadcrumbs. Then add the juice and mix into a dough.

Divide into 2 portions and place half on a greased non-stick oven tray. Spread it out over the tray by hand, leaving a small border free all around the edges. Fill with the fruit and then cover with the rest of the dough, by distributing it in small clumps and melding together with the back of a fork, until it covers all the fruit.

Bake at gas 4 / 350°F for 30 mins, turning halfway through the cooking time. Cut into 16 pieces.

Muesli Squares

150g / 1½ cups of oat flakes (not jumbo or whole oats)
150g / 1⅛ cups of strong whole wheat flour
dashes of salt
30g / ⅓ cup of desiccated coconut
150g / 1¼ cups of mixed dried fruit chopped small
30g / ⅓ cup of chopped hazelnuts
30g / ⅓ cup of sunflower seeds
100g / ½ cup of vegetable fat spread
300ml / 1¼ cups of apple juice

Mix all the above together (except the apple juice) using your fingers, until like muesli clusters. Add the juice and mix in.

Grease a non stick oven tray and cover with the mixture, pressing well down, leaving a small margin clear around the edges. Bake at gas 4 / 350°F for 30 minutes turning halfway through the cooking time. Cut into 16 pieces.

Oat Buns

150g / 1½ cups of oatflakes (not jumbo or whole oats)
150g / 1⅛ cups of strong whole wheat flour
2 teaspoons of bicarbonate of soda
dashes of salt
125g / 1 cup of finely chopped dates
35g / ¼ cup of root ginger finely chopped
100g / ½ cup of vegetable fat spread
250ml / 1 cup of apple juice

Mix all the above together (except the juice) using your fingers until like coarse breadcrumbs. Add the apple juice and mix well in.

Grease a non-stick, 12 place, deep bun tray and fill with the mixture. Bake at gas 3 / 325°F for 30 minutes turning halfway through the cooking time.

Peanut Butter Brownies

Just right with a mug of coffee.

  50g / ¼ cup of vegetable fat spread
  100g / ¼lb of high quality plain chocolate
  125g / ½ cup of crunchy peanut butter
  sprinkling of salt if none in the peanut butter
  180ml / ¾ cup of apple juice
  150g / 1⅛ cups of strong whole wheat flour
  1½ teaspoons of bicarbonate of soda
  75g / ½ cup of raisins

Very gently melt the fat and chocolate in a pan; then turn off the heat. Add the peanut butter mixing in thoroughly with the back of a fork. Then add the apple juice and stir well in.

Place the flour, bicarb and raisins in a bowl and mix together using your fingers. Add the liquid ingredients and blend in with a wooden spoon.

Grease a non-stick oven tray and place the mixture in the centre. Make into a 20mm / ¾ inch high block. Bake at gas 4 / 350°F for 18 minutes, turning the tray halfway through the cooking time. Cut into 12 pieces.

Rich Fruit Cake

For those special occasions.

>250g / 2 cups of whole wheat strong flour
>sprinkling of salt
>1 teaspoon each of cinnamon, nutmeg and cloves
>100g / ½ cup of vegetable fat spread
>175g / 1¼ cups of sultanas / golden raisins
>175g / 1¼ cups of raisins
>175g / 1¼ cups of figs chopped small (remove any
>hard stems)
>1 large orange (use the zest and the juice)
>1 lemon (use the zest and the juice)
>250ml / 1 cup of apple juice
>greaseproof paper
>small packet of flaked almonds

Mix the flour, salt, spices and fat together using your fingers, until breadcrumb like. Add the dried fruit; then add the orange and lemon zests and juices, plus the apple juice. Mix everything together very thoroughly using your fingers.

Grease a 22cm / 8¾ inch, oblong non-stick tin, then line this with greaseproof paper. Trim off any excess paper, as it is not flameproof. Then grease the paper very thoroughly and place the cake mixture in the tin, smoothing it out. Decorate the top with enough flaked almonds to completely cover the surface, pressing down well.

Bake for 1 hour 40 minutes at gas 2½ / 312°F, turning the tin halfway through the cooking time.

When the cake has cooled take it out of the tin and gently remove the paper. Wrap it in fresh greaseproof paper and place in a plastic container with the lid on.

Leave for 2 days before eating to allow the flavours to mature and the cake to set. As no eggs are used the cake should be cut gently into thickish slices to avoid crumbling.

This cake will keep for 1 month but the flavours are at their best in the first fortnight.

Scones

300g / 2¼ cups of strong whole wheat flour
dashes of salt
2 teaspoons of bicarbonate of soda
100g / ¾ cup of raisins
100g / ½ cup of vegetable fat spread
250ml / 1 cup of apple juice

Mix all the above together (except the juice) using your fingers, until breadcrumb like. Then add the apple juice and mix well in.

Divide the mix into 12-16 blobs using a tablespoon and place on a greased non-stick oven tray. Bake at gas 3 / 325ºF for 30 minutes turning halfway through the cooking time.

Tofucake

An enjoyable high-protein dessert.

Makes 6 portions
175g / 1⅛ cups of strong whole wheat flour
sprinkling of salt
1 teaspoon of bicarbonate of soda
75g / ⅓ cup of vegetable fat spread
160ml / ⅔ cup of apple juice
280g / 1¾ cups of tofu cubed
3 tablespoons of raisins
6 tablespoons of ground almonds
200g / ¾ cup of commercial fruit spread of choice,
a type sweetened with fruit juice
small packet of chopped hazels
500g / 2 cups of natural soya yoghurt

Mix the first 4 ingredients together using your fingers, until breadcrumb like. Then add 80ml / ⅓ cup of apple juice and mix in.

Place the dough in a greased, 20cm / 8 inch non-stick flan dish, and press down and up the sides with your fingers. Bake for 20mins at gas 6 / 400°F, turning halfway through the cooking time.

Meanwhile, place the tofu, a sprinkling of salt and 80ml / ⅓ cup of apple juice in a bowl and mash with a fork until mushy. Then add the raisins and ground almonds and mix well in.

When the base is cooked place the fruit spread over it. Cover with the tofu mixture, sprinkling by hand evenly, and smooth out with the back of a fork. Sprinkle a coating of the chopped hazels evenly over the top and press down lightly with a fork.

Leave for at least a few hours before eating and serve topped with the yoghurt.

Fruit Trifle

Serves 4
4 thin slices of fruit cake or scone
fresh fruit of choice, e.g. 4 nectarines sliced or
equivalent strawberries or raspberries or a mixture of fruits
500ml / 2 cups of pure fruit juice
1 tablespoon Gelozone (or another unflavoured vegan
thickener like Agar Agar, following the instructions on
the packet)
small carton of vegan cream

Share the cake between 4 small dishes. Prepare the fruit and place over
the cake.

Pour the fruit juice into a pan and sprinkle evenly with the Gelozone,
then mix it in. Bring to boil stirring constantly, remove from the heat as
soon as it bubbles. Pour a quarter of the jelly over the top of each dish;
allow to cool.

Serve with the cream.

Summer Pudding

This recipe is easy to make and after marination, turns into a very fruity and refreshing sponge pudding.

Serves 6
large rounds of medium sliced whole wheat bread with
the crusts cut off (see below for the amount needed)
1200g / 2lb 10oz of strawberries or raspberries or
other soft fruit
2 tablespoons of muscavado sugar
medium carton of soya cream
large, round, deep, straight sided dish
heavy object placed on top of a plate which then fits
fairly snugly inside the dish

Put enough water in a medium sized pan to just cover the bottom, then add the fruit. Place the lid on and steam for 4 minutes with the heat at full blast. Then remove from the heat and stir in the sugar. Refrigerate 1 large mug of the fruit and its juice.

Cover the bottom and sides of the large round dish with the bread, slightly overlapping it. Pour the fruit and juice from the pan into the centre of the bread. Fold the tops of the bread down onto the fruit and cover with another piece of bread if there are gaps. Place the plate and heavy object on top so that they press the pudding; refrigerate overnight.

The next day gently slip a knife round the sides of the pudding, then turn the dish upside down and ease the pudding onto a plate. Cut into 6 portions; serve topped with the remaining fruit and juice plus the cream.

Summertime Treat

A handy snack meal for any time of the day.

Serves 2
1 mug / 1 cup of oatflakes or whole oats (not jumbo)
sprinkling of salt
1 mug / 1 cup of malted crispy wheat flakes
1 large banana or nectarine chopped small or other
fresh fruit of choice
½ mug / ½ cup of soya milk
½ mug / ½ cup of water
6 tablespoons of natural soya yoghurt

Take 2 large bowls and divide the dry ingredients and fruit between them. Mix all well in together.

Add the milk and water and top with the yoghurt, dividing equally. Serve immediately.

Baked Pears
with Chocolate Sauce

Serves 4
4 medium sized conference pears (they are ripe when
the end near the stem is softish when squeezed) trim
off the ends and slice down the middle, scoop out any
seeds with a teaspoon
2 tablespoons of vegetable fat spread
100g / ¼lb of best quality plain chocolate
small carton of apple juice
small packet of chopped hazelnuts
small carton of natural soya yoghurt

Grease 4 small oval oven dishes and place the pears in them, cut side up.
Bake at gas 7 / 425°F for 20 minutes, turning the dishes and swapping
shelves halfway through the cooking time.

When the pears are almost ready, melt the fat and chocolate very slowly
in a pan stirring constantly. Then gradually add the apple juice stirring as
you do so, until the sauce is the thickness you would like. Then continue
to heat through until the sauce gently bubbles.

Immediately pour the sauce over the pears. Then sprinkle a few of the
chopped nuts over each dish. Serve with the yoghurt.

Pear Delight

A delicious way to enjoy pears.

Serves 6
6 medium sized ripe conference pears (they are ripe
when the end near the stem is softish when squeezed)
trim off both ends and slice down the middle, scoop
out any seeds with a teaspoon
200g / 1½ cups of strong whole wheat flour
sprinkling of salt
100g / ½ cup of vegetable fat spread
small packet of chopped hazelnuts
500g / 2 cups of natural soya yoghurt

Place the pears cut side up, in 6 small oven dishes along with 200ml /
¾ cup of water divided up between them.

Weigh out the flour, add the salt and vegetable fat and mix all together
using your fingers, until breadcrumb like.

Cover the pears with the crumble mix and sprinkle the hazels over
the top.

Bake at gas 5 / 375ºF for 30 minutes, turning the dishes and swapping
shelves halfway through the cooking time. Serve with the yoghurt.

Apple Charlotte

Serves 4
4 small oval oven dishes
enough slices of medium thickness whole wheat bread
to fit into the dishes to make 3 layers
vegetable fat spread
4 large strong flavoured dessert apples or equivalent
baking apples sliced small
8 tablespoons of sugar free vegan mincemeat
small carton of natural soya yoghurt

Spread the vegetable fat thinly over both sides of the bread. Cut the bread up to fit into the dishes.

Place one layer of bread at the bottom of each dish and cover with half of the apple pieces and half of the mincemeat. Place another layer of bread over the fruit and then the rest of the apple pieces and mincemeat. Finish with the rest of the bread.

Put 200ml / 1 cup of water in a jug and pour a quarter of this over the top of each charlotte, soaking the top slice of bread as you do so.

Bake at gas 5 / 375ºF for 30 minutes, turning the dishes and swapping shelves halfway through the cooking time.

Needs to be eaten warm; serve with the yoghurt.

Rice Pudding

A new slant on an old favourite.

Serves 4 to 6
200g / 1 cup of whole short grain rice
dashes of salt

Place the above in a large pan with 500ml / 2 cups of water, then bring to boil. Place the lid on and simmer very gently for 35 minutes, by which time all the water should be absorbed and the rice cooked.

500ml / 2 cups of soya milk
8 tablespoons of ground almonds
14 dried dates cut up finely
1 teaspoon of ground nutmeg

Add the above to the cooked rice along with 150ml / 2/3 cup of water, mixing well in. Bring to boil, then simmer for approximately 20 minutes with the lid on, by which time it should be a creamy texture.

Apple or Rhubarb Crumble

Serves 6
150g / 1½ cups of oatflakes (not jumbo or whole oats)
150g / 1⅛ cups of strong whole wheat flour
dashes of salt
100g / ½ cup of vegetable fat spread
carton of soya custard

Filling A: 6 large strong flavoured dessert apples or
3 large cooking apples chopped small
options: sprinkling of raisins, blackberries or finely
chopped lemon

or

Filling B: 600g / 1½lb of rhubarb, not peeled but
chopped small, discard ends
6 tablespoons of muscavado sugar

Mix the oats, flour, salt and vegetable fat together using your fingers, until like coarse breadcrumbs.

Place the apples or rhubarb in 6 small oven dishes along with 300ml / 1¼ cups of water divided up between each dish.

If using apples sprinkle with any of the options desired; raisins go well with cooking apples.

If using rhubarb sprinkle with the muscavado.

Sprinkle the crumble mix over the top of each dish and bake at gas 5 / 375ºF for 30 minutes, turning the dishes and swapping shelves halfway through the cooking time.

Serve with the custard.

Baked Bananas
with Chocolate Sauce

Yummy and easy to make.

Serves 4
4 medium sized bananas peeled
2 tablespoons of vegetable fat spread
100g / ¼ lb of best quality plain chocolate
small carton of apple juice
small packet of chopped hazelnuts
small carton of natural soya yoghurt

Proceed as in the baked pear recipe on page 176 but leave the bananas whole.

Banana & Lemon Charlotte

Serves 4

4 small oval oven dishes
enough slices of medium thickness whole wheat bread
to fit into the dishes to make 3 layers
vegetable fat spread
3 medium bananas sliced into rounds
2 slices of lemon finely chopped
small carton of chocolate soya custard

Spread the vegetable fat thinly over both sides of the bread. Cut the bread up to fit into the dishes.

Place one layer of bread at the bottom of each dish and cover with half of the banana slices, then sprinkle with half of the lemon bits. Place more bread over the fruit and then the rest of the banana and lemon, finishing with the rest of the bread.

Fill a jug with 200ml / ¾ cup of water and pour a quarter of this over the top of each Charlotte, soaking the top slice of bread as you do so.

Bake at gas 4 / 350°F for 30 minutes, turning the dishes and swapping shelves halfway through the cooking time. Needs to be eaten warm. Serve with the custard.

Muscavado & Lemon Pancakes

Scrumptious and filling.

> **Serves 4**
> 200g / 1⅓ cups of strong whole wheat flour
> dashes of salt
> small packet of muscavado sugar
> juice of 1½ lemons
> 300g / 1¼ cups of natural soya yoghurt

Weigh out the flour, add the salt, and gradually mix in 500ml / 2¼ cups of water, smoothing out any lumps.

Use a small non-stick cast iron frying pan, or part of a medium one. Oil the pan and heat it through for a couple of minutes at a little under medium heat.

Add 1/8 of the batter to the pan, distributing it evenly by gripping the pan handle with both hands and tilting from side to side. Fry until the underside is golden brown, about 2 or 3 minutes; then turn and do the other side which will cook quicker.

Whilst still cooking the second side sprinkle lightly with the muscavado and ⅛ of the lemon juice. When the pancake is cooked fold one side into the centre, then the other side to the centre, slightly overlapping the first side.

Lay out 4 small oven dishes and place the pancake in one; then cook another and place it at the side of the first. Pop them in the oven to keep warm. Repeat the process until you have made 8 pancakes. Top with the yoghurt and serve.

INDEX